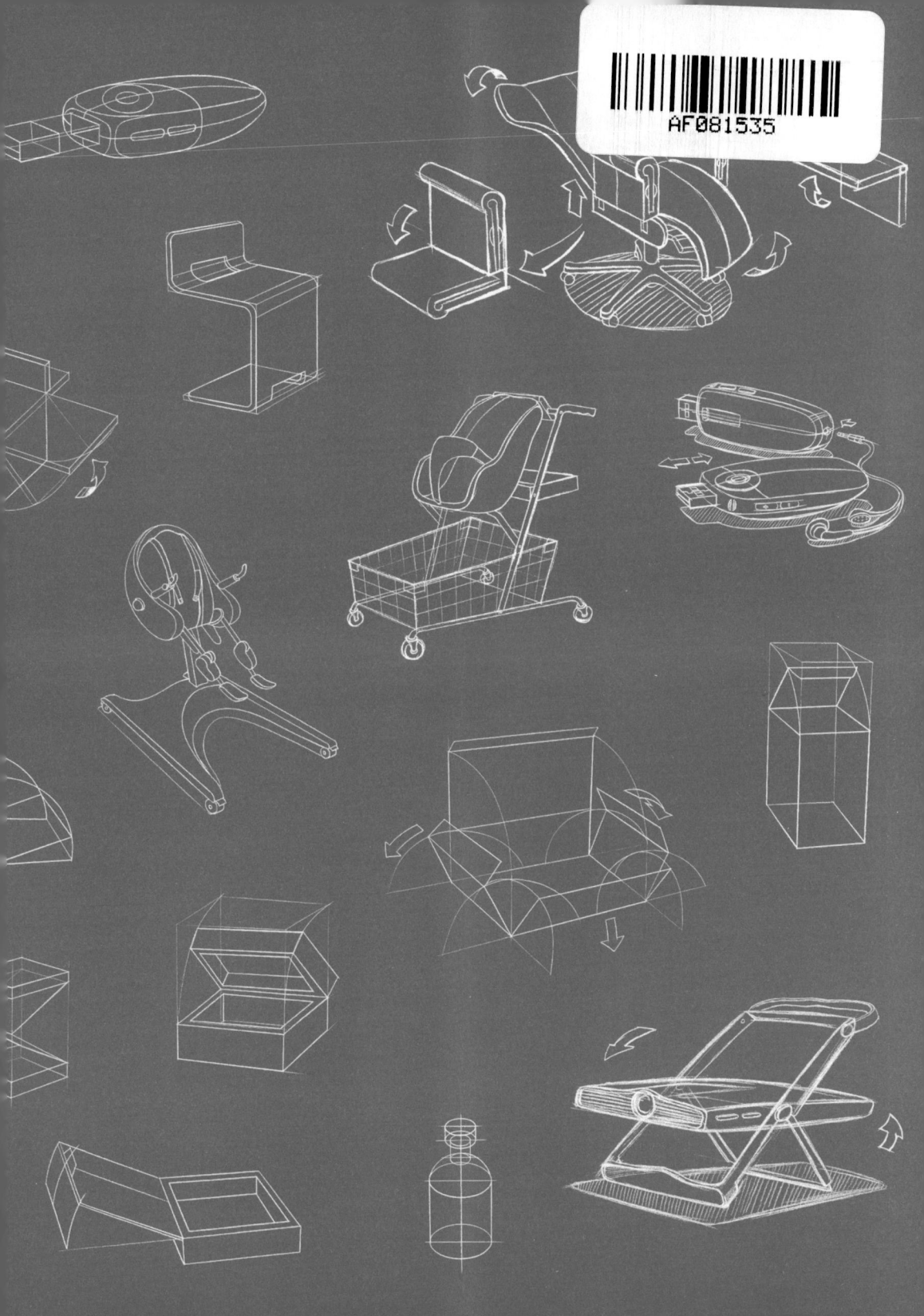

SKETCH LIKE A PRO

Detailed Step-by-step Tutorial with 450 Sketching Samples

Li Fengyan

PRODUCT DESIGN SKETCHING TECHNIQUE AND PRESENTATION

sendpoints

SKETCH LIKE A PRO
PRODUCT DESIGN SKETCHING TECHNIQUE AND PRESENTATION

Text and Images © Li Fengyan
Original Copyright © Guangxi Fine Arts Publishing House Co., Ltd
English Edition © 2021 Sendpoints Publishing Co., Ltd.
First printing of the first edition, July 2021

sendpoints

PUBLISHED BY Sendpoints Publishing Co., Ltd.
PUBLISHER: Lin Gengli
PUBLISHING DIRECTOR : Nicole Lo
CHIEF EDITOR: Nicole Lo
EXECUTIVE EDITOR: Wenyin Chen , Qiumei Lin
DESIGN DIRECTOR: Dongyan Wu
EXECUTIVE ART EDITOR: Peng Zhenwei Design Office
PROOFREADER: Wenyin Chen , Chujun Huang

REGISTERED ADDRESS: Room 15A Block 9 Tsui Chuk Garden, Wong Tai Sin, Kowloon, Hong Kong, China
TEL: +852-35832323 / **FAX:** +852-35832448
OFFICE ADDRESS: 7F, No.9-1 Anning Street, Jinshazhou Road, Baiyun District, Guangzhou, China
TEL: +86-20-89095121 / **FAX:** +86-20-89095206
BEIJING OFFICE: Room 513, 5th Floor, Building 1, Longde Zijinjia, No.186 Litang Road, Changping District, Beijing, China
TEL: +86-10-84139071 / **FAX:** +86-10-84139071
SHANGHAI OFFICE: Room 302, Floor 3, Ningbo Road no.349, Huangpu District, Shanghai, China
TEL: +86-21-63523469 / **FAX:** +86-21-63523469

SALES DIRECTOR: Philip Tsang
TEL: +86-20-81007895
EMAIL: sales@sendpoints.cn
WEBSITE: www.sendpoints.cn / www.spbooks.cn

ISBN 978-988-74767-6-4

All rights reserved. No part of this publication may be reproduced, stored in a retrieval system or transmitted in any form or by any means, electronic, mechanical, photocopying, recording or otherwise, without prior permission in writing from the publisher. For more information, please contact Sendpoints Publishing Co., Ltd.
Printed and bound in China.

CONTENTS

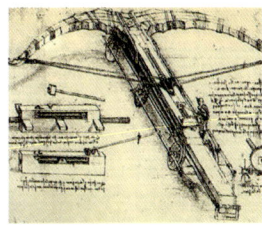

005
Chapter 1
Introduction

017
Chapter 2
Preparation for Perspective, Principle of Composition and Tools

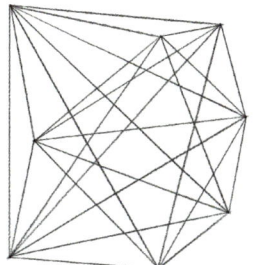

041
Chapter 3
Basics of Expression Techniques

063
Chapter 4
Expression Techniques of Product Material

113
Chapter 5
Instance Analysis of Product Modeling Design

Introduction

CHAPTER 1

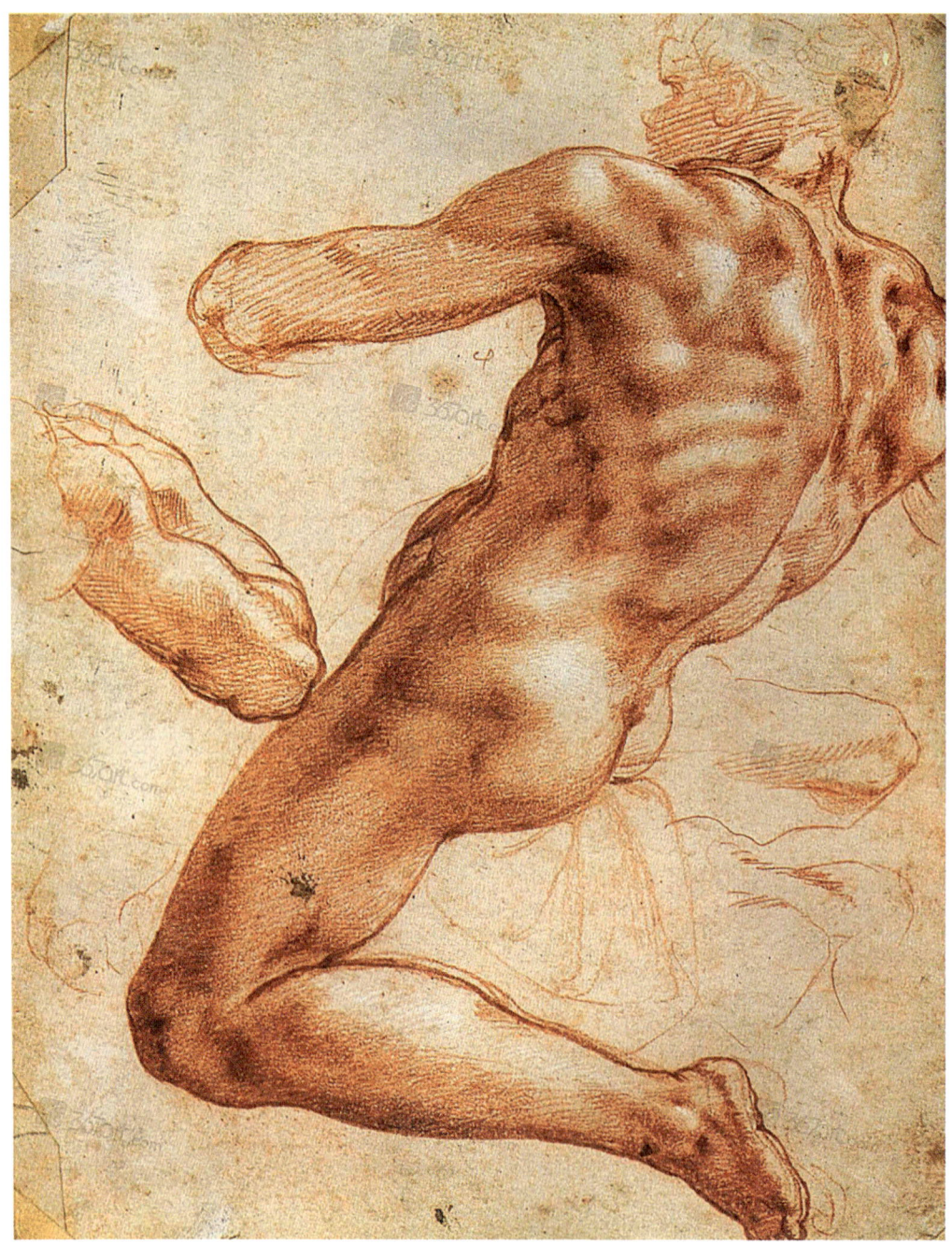

Fig.1.1 Hand-drawn sketch of a human figure by Michelangelo

Hand drawing is a freehand technique used to draw patterns, and has applications in various fields. Its origins can be traced to the European Renaissance era. The art of hand drawing has a long history, and was mainly used in structural engineering and anatomical schematics. The most prominent ones were created by maestros, such as Michelangelo, Leonardo da Vinci and Raffaello Santi. They used hand-drawn sketches to reflect and present their creative designs, as shown in Fig.1.1 to Fig.1.4. It is said that "Rome was not built in a day". Rigorous hand-drawing skills can only be acquired through learning sound drawing techniques and continuous practise.

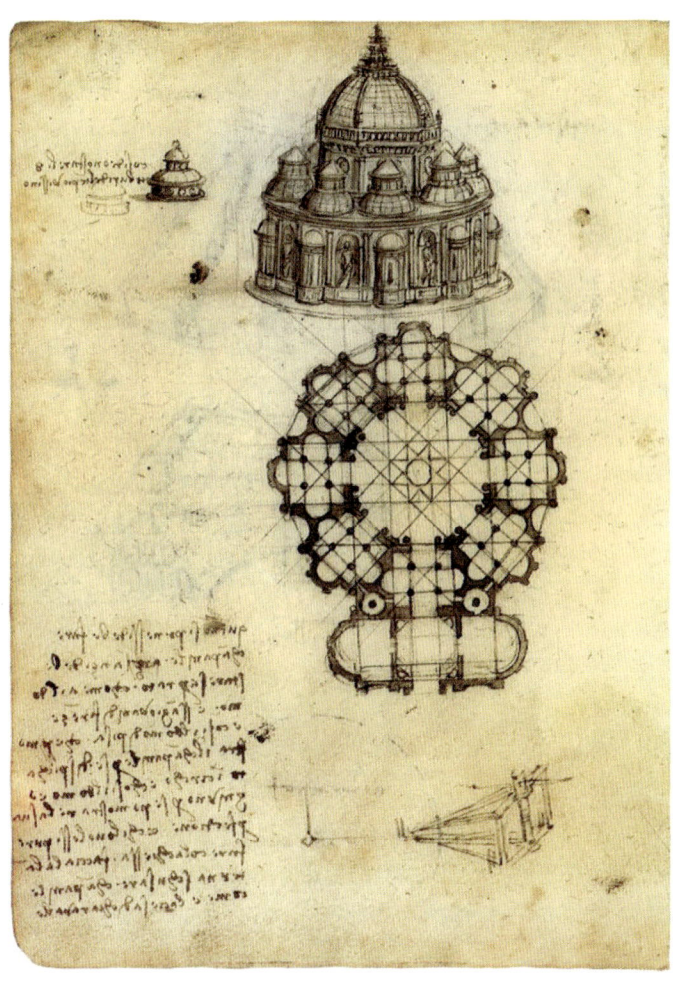

Fig.1.2　Hand-drawn architectural sketch by Leonardo da Vinci

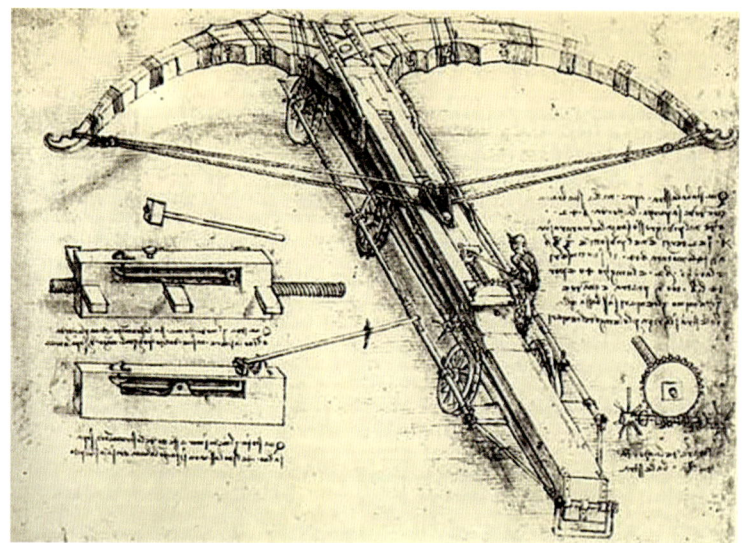

Fig.1.3 Leonardo da Vinci's sketch of one of his mechanical inventions

Fig.1.4 Hand-drawn composition by Raffaello Santi

Fig.1.5 Creating a sketch

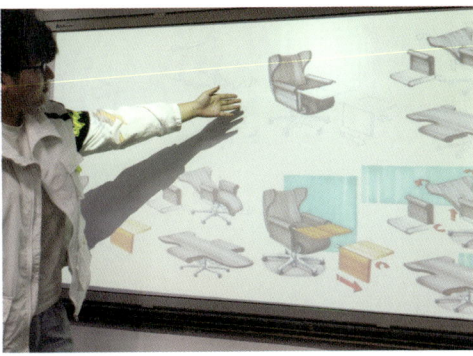
Fig.1.6 Reviewing a proposed sketch

The 21st century is the information age, the network age, and the digital age. Many people have questioned the relevance of this traditional form of hand drawing. They opine that in these times, it is outdated for designers to use hand-drawn sketches to showcase their work and that they should adopt the more convenient computer graphics. Some even believe that hand drawing should be relegated to history. However, we find the opposite trend in corporate design departments and campus design studios. Many designers and beginners still use hand drawing or sketches to present various product modeling designs. Hand drawing is still irreplaceable. The reason behind the popularity of hand drawing techniques is their deep connections with multiple disciplines such as architectural design, fashion design, garden design, environmental art design, product design, and visual communication design. Over time, hand drawing techniques have evolved to cater to the needs of designing in several fields. Professionals such as architects, advertising designers, design researchers, have specialized in applying these, and there are distinctive and professional industry norms. For people in the design industry, working on their hand drawing techniques is a life-long process throughout their careers. It is also one of the essential compulsory courses for design majors and a key professional skill to master, as shown in Fig.1.5 and Fig.1.6.

Overview of Product Modeling Design

Definition of products

Any goods created and produced by human beings to meet their needs are called products. Over time, people have gained a deeper understanding of products, which include not only tangible goods, but also intangible services, layouts and concepts. From the perspective of industrial design, products refer to a variety of mass-produced physical objects used by consumers, from small buttons and pencils to cars and airplanes.

Every product has two forms, the internal form and the external one. The internal form mainly defined by technical aspects such as material, structure, and process, is the basis for the external form of the product. The external form is mainly presented through modeling. In addition to meeting the functional requirements of the product, the characteristics of the product interact with users' senses such as vision, hearing, touch and smell to create a unique user experience. In this way, the product is utilitarian as well as appreciated.

Definition of product design

Product design takes place in all creative human activities. It is a series of behavior by which human labor and tools transform and rebuild nature to provide for daily necessities and improve the living environment. Product design is a closely related to production methods, and is a comprehensive process that integrates product function, materials, structure, technology, form, color, surface treatment, decoration, and other factors. From the perspective of society, economy and technology, product design should not only meet people's requirements of the utility of the product, but also address users' aesthetic needs. It is a creative activity that organically combines factors like science, art, culture, economy, society, and so on. Product design represents one of the subcategories of industrial design. It plays a significant role in industrial design, which reflects the economic development, technology, and culture of an era. Good product design is the key to win customers. Many industrial design companies in developed countries regard product design as a crucial strategic development tool and invest hugely in design to gain an added advantage in the competitive market for new popular products. Overall, a successful product design is expected to lead social and cultural development, improve product function, quality, and efficiency, and more importantly, meet the usage requirements or improve the manufacturing processes. Therefore, product design is about making products more suitable for people, and its ultimate goal is to meet humans' utilitarian needs.

Fig.1.7 A sketching work area

Definition of product modeling design

Considering the materials, structure, and processing methods of the product, product modeling design turns out to be the detailed design of the product's function, rationality, economy, and aesthetics. A three-dimensional design of the product is created keeping in mind several perspectives such as aesthetics, natural science, economics and engineering technology, and other aspects.

Product modeling design aims to perfectly combine the technical aspects and functionality of the product with its aesthetic aspect. This not only reflects the value in the use of the product and meets certain material functional requirements, but also addresses the aesthetic needs of the user to achieve a personalized product experience. We have to bear in mind that a product that is rationally structured to be functional may not be aesthetically pleasing when modeled.

Purpose and significance of product modeling design expression

Expression is to visualize abstract concepts and complex language. Design is a creative act as well as an artistic expression, which concretely represents people's pursuit of asethetics. While designing products, product modeling design expression also reflects the appeal and permeability of art, showcasing the conception and creation of the design through rich imagination and creativity. It is the best combination of practicality and art. Design cannot be separated from expression. Design expression, a direct visual image language, is the detailed presentation of the product's function, shape, material, color, etc. Specific graphics can enhance the design creativity. Product modeling design expression, a professional form of applied drawing, has become a prerequisite expertise for designers, as shown in Fig.1.7 and Fig.1.8. It not only accurately expresses the designer's design concept, but also reflects the

Introduction **011**

designer's creativity, artistic accomplishment, and personality.

In modern design education, students are taught to observe, think, analyze, and solve specific problems in design practise to improve their professional design ability. The training enables them to become professional designers by acquiring systematic professional knowledge and strict training in professional skills. The advantages of hand drawing are that it can directly convey the designer's design concept, visually present the product, and clearly explain the design intention on paper. The charm of hand-drawing lies in the strong visual impact it creates on the viewer with the skillful use of expression techniques. It is obvious that hand drawing techniques in product modeling design are vitally essential to become a prominent designer, as a good design stems from skilled and expressive hand-drawing.

Fig.1. 8 Example of a hand-drawn sketch of a product

Classifications of Product Modeling Design and Characteristics of Expression Techniques

Classifications of product modeling design

There are products designed to meet every possible material need and the variety of products in demand have been increasing along with the development of society, economy, and culture. From the perspective of product modeling design, industrial design products can be divided into 10 main categories:

1. Electronics and communications—TVs, DVs, digital cameras, video cameras, remote control devices, desk telephones, mobile phones, fax machines, recorders, audio devices and, etc.

2. Computers and accessories—Desktop computers, laptop computers, keyboard, mouse, USB flash drives, mobile HDD (mobile hard disk drive), external webcams, gamepads, printers, copiers, monitors, scanners, optical lanterns, projectors, wireless routers, etc.

3. Office products—Office desk and chair, conference room table and chair, file cabinet, stationery, cultural and recreational products, etc.

4. Lighting products—Indoor and outdoor lighting fixtures and accessories.

5. Home and living Products—Household appliances, kitchen items, tableware, sanitary and bathroom equipment, home decoration and accessories, etc.

6. Leisure and fashion—Outdoor goods, sporting goods, fitness equipment, playground equipment, garden tools, gaming devices, baby products, fashion clothing, glasses, jewelry, watches, leather accessories, instruments, optical goods, etc.

7. Industrial and construction facilities—Production equipment, power tools, factory facilities, measuring tools, sanitary equipment, heating equipment, security equipment, windows, doors, balconies, awnings, handrails, roofs, greenhouses, garages, solar energy equipment, fireplaces, etc.

8. Medical and health assistance—Medical instruments, medical office, laboratory equipment, BADL (Basic Activities of Daily Living) devices, rehabilitation facilities, etc.

9. Public facilities—Restaurants, shops, lounges, libraries, museums, amusement facilities, display facilities, shopping facilities, outdoor billboards, bus and tram stop equipment, etc.

10. Transport—Bicycles, electric bicycles, motorcycles, balance bikes, sedans, sports cars, SUVs (sport utility vehicles), MPVs (multipurpose vehicles), buses, agricultural vehicles, construction vehicles, railway vehicles, aircrafts, ships, etc.

Characteristics of expression techniques in product modeling design

Expression means displayed behavior, speech, style, and ideas, which can be presented by writing, speaking, and drawing. Expression, in this book, refers to the drawing technique, which visualizes the design concept to showcase the product's modeling, structure, material, color, function, and process in two-dimensional or three-dimensional drawing forms. The expression of product modeling design is the process of making the product vivid, detailed and concrete through visual images so that designer's ideas are communicated to others easily.

A product needs to have a channel by which designers can communicate and exchange their design ideas throughout the whole process from conceptualizing and research and development to production and marketing. Product design renderings have become a universally recognized communication method due to their advantages of being intuitive, vivid, and easy-to-understand. During the whole product design process, basic information like appearance, internal structure, processing technology and materials are communicated, and each department is linked to the others via product design renderings. This enables personnel from design, technology, production, and sales departments to understand the product comprehensively with its design scheme.

Product modeling design rendering, resulting from design ideas and creative expressions, is an indispensable basic skill that designers have to master. An effective product modeling design rendering should possess the following characteristics.

1. Authenticity
The real effect of the product is presented through color, texture, and artistic treatment. The foremost meaning of product renderings is to convey genuine and true product

Fig.1.9 Creating a sketch

Fig.1.10 Presenting a sketch

information, so that performances of new products and the real effects in a certain environment can be understood.

2. Illustration

As a saying goes, "A picture speaks louder than a thousand words." This means graphics are more expressive than words. Product renderings not only fully represent the form, structure, color, and texture of the product, but also convey the designer's pursuit of beauty in product design.

3. Aesthetics

The design rendering is more than a product instruction. Its aesthetic features should arouse viewers' interest and resonate with their sensibilities, reflecting abstract contents such as intangible rhythm, shapes, and aesthetics.

4. Convenience

When presenting a design to a client, the designer often receives suggestions from the client, which must be incorporated and represented graphically. This can be done in a relatively short period of time with renderings, which are more convenient than physical models and computer renderings, as shown in Fig.1.9 and Fig.1.10.

In general, product design rendering is an essential step in the design process as it records the inspiration and creative ideas of designers and serves as an effective tool for communication between designers and customers. Therefore, it is important to learn product design rendering techniques.

Preparation for Perspective, Principle of Composition and Tools

CHAPTER 2

Overview of Perspective Principle

It is assumed that a transparent plane exists between the object and the observer, the intersection points of the observer's sight lines and the plane need to be connected to form a pattern. Perspective refers to drawing the projection of the spatial object on the plane with the observer's eye at the center.

Perspective is a technique of representing an object three-dimensionally on a two-dimensional plane by using graphical perspective principles and using geometric drawing techniques. The images of identical objects in our retina vary with distance and position. For instance, objects of the same size and width appear smaller and lower as their distance from the observer increases. This is one of the most common perspective phenomena.

Perspective plays a significant role in industrial design. It is one of the basic skills of a designer. It is a fundamental creative technique that enables accurate rendering of freehand drawings, making the sketch look realistic and technical while offering a sense of depth. The principle of perspective is a prerequisite for accurate hand-drawing sketches.

Characteristics of perspective: Objects appear smaller, lower and shorter as the distance between the observers and the objects increases.

Common terms in understanding perspective:

1. Eye Point (E)—The position of the observer's eyes.

2. Horizon Line (HL)—A horizontal line at the same level of eyes.

3. Center of Vision (CV)—The intersection point, where the line that emerges from the eye point perpendicular to the horizon line meets the horizon line, also called central point.

4. Vanishing Point (VP)—A point on the image plane where projection points of parallel lines converge.

5. Central Visual Ray (CVR)—The vertical line from eye point to the image plane, the central axis of vision cone, also known as central line of sight.

6. Ground Line (GL)—The intersection line of the picture plane (usually vertical) and the ground plane (usually horizontal).

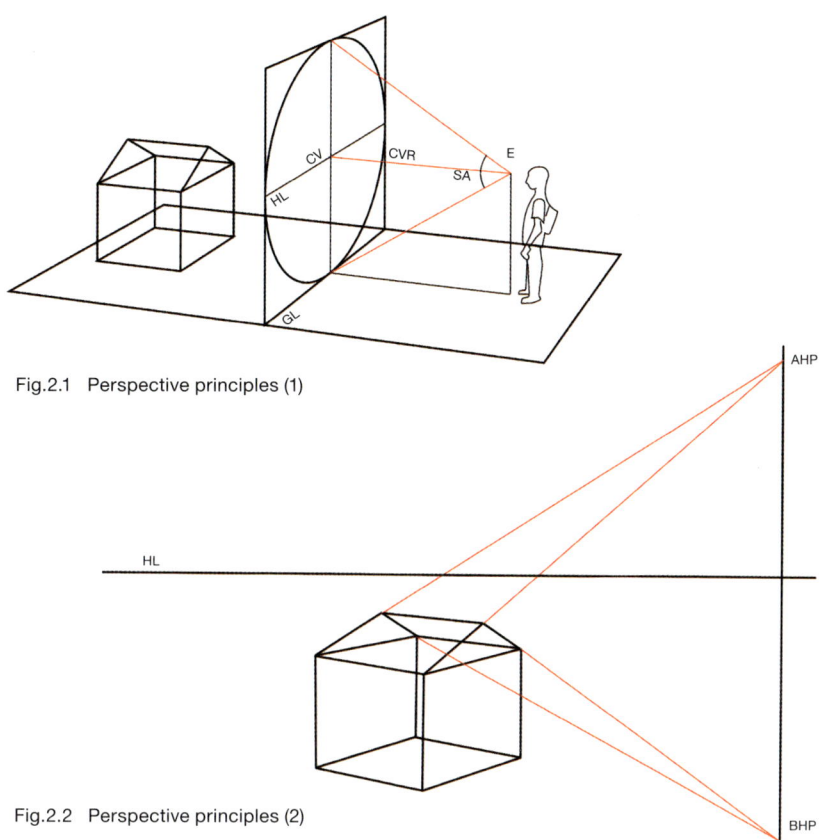

Fig.2.1 Perspective principles (1)

Fig.2.2 Perspective principles (2)

7. Sight Angle (SA)—The angle between any two sight lines that start from the eye point. Sight angle is ususally 60°.

8. Above Horizontal Point (AHP)—The vanishing point from the tilted-upward line that is not parallel to the plane.

9. Below Horizontal Point (BHP)—The vanishing point from the tilted-downward line that is not parallel to the plane.

These terms are illustrated in Fig.2.1 and Fig.2.2.

Perspective is often categorized as one-point perspective (parallel perspective), two-point perspective (angular perspective) and three-point perspective (oblique perspective) in product drawing. To ensure the quality of drawing, perspective must be mastered proficiently.

One-point perspective

One-point perspective is also called parallel perspective. Take a cube as an example. When the front and the back sides of the cube are parallel to the image plane, the extension of lines of the other sides that are perpendicular to the image plane converge at a single point (a vanishing point) on the horizon line. This is called one-point perspective. One-point perspective is a popular perspective method in product hand drawing due to its advantages—it is relatively simple, creating an illusion of depth and neat and whole, as shown in Fig.2.3 to Fig.2.6.

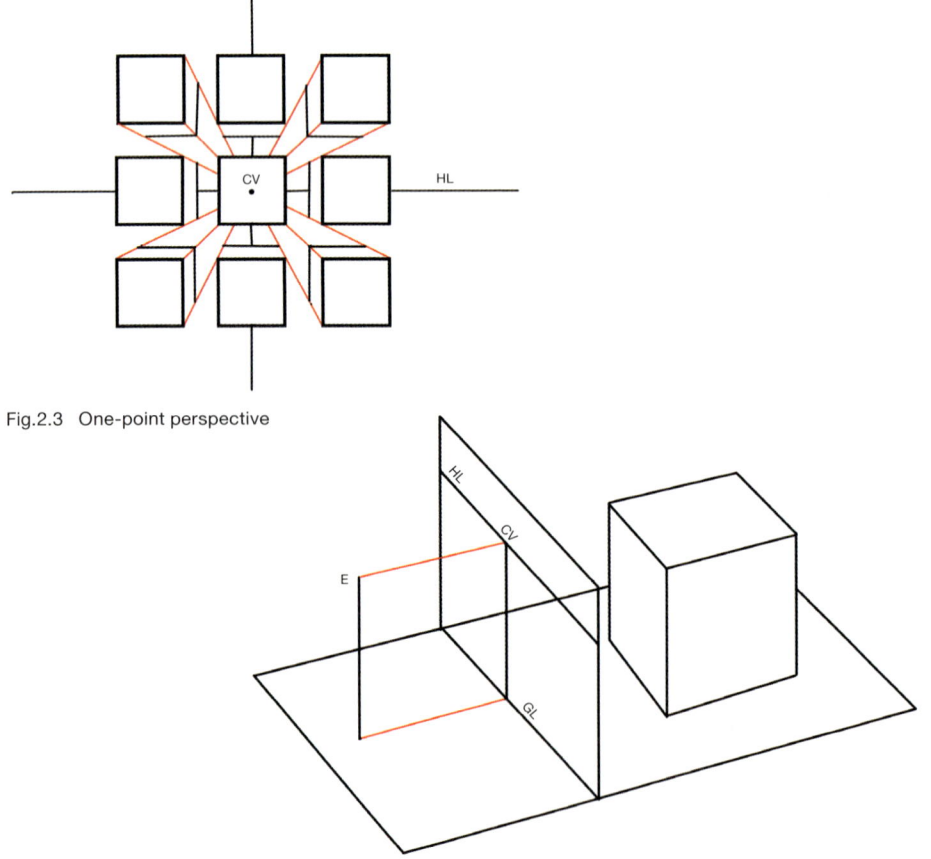

Fig.2.3 One-point perspective

Fig.2.4 Principles of one-point perspective

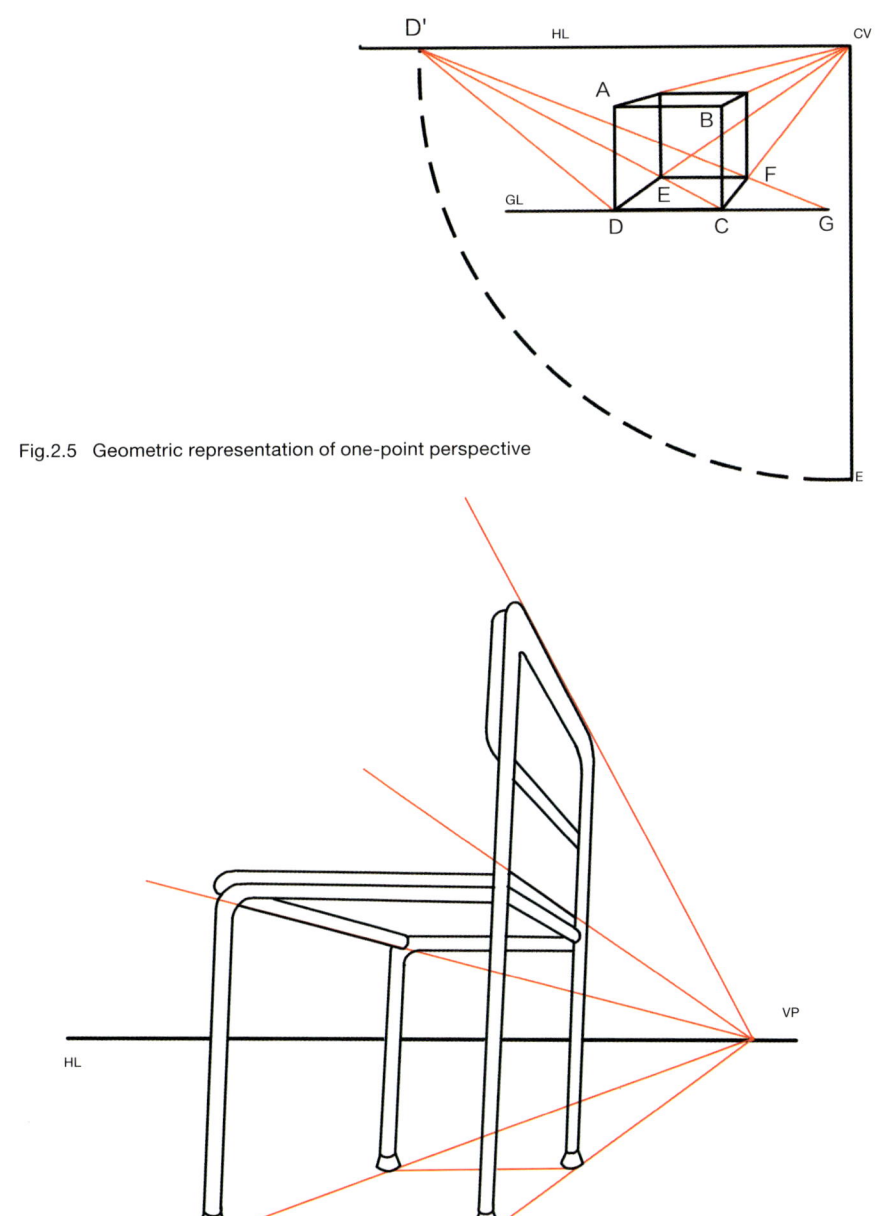

Fig.2.5 Geometric representation of one-point perspective

Fig.2.6 Example of one-point perspective of a chair

Preparation for Perspective, Principle of Composition and Tools

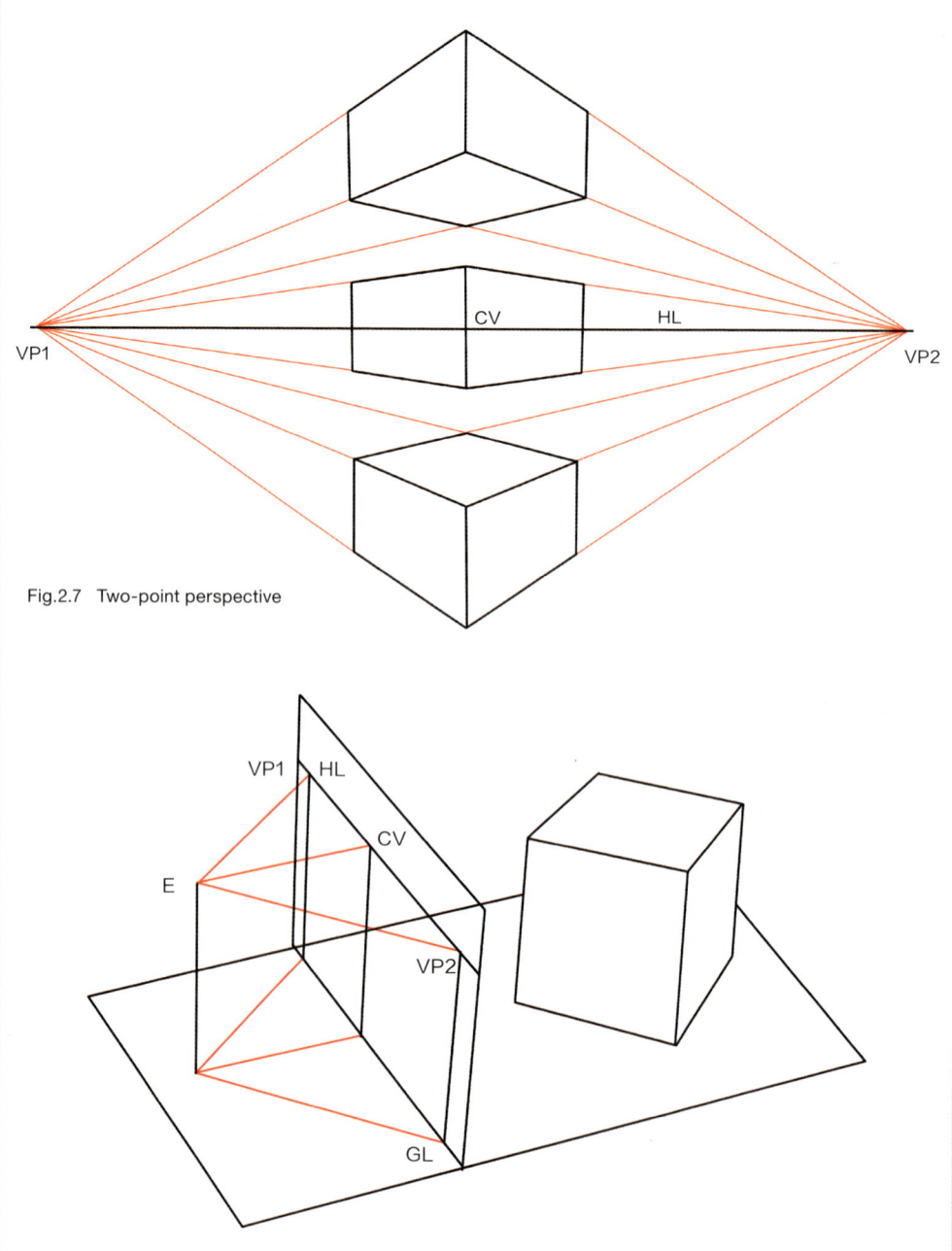

Fig.2.7 Two-point perspective

Fig.2.8 Principles of two-point perspective

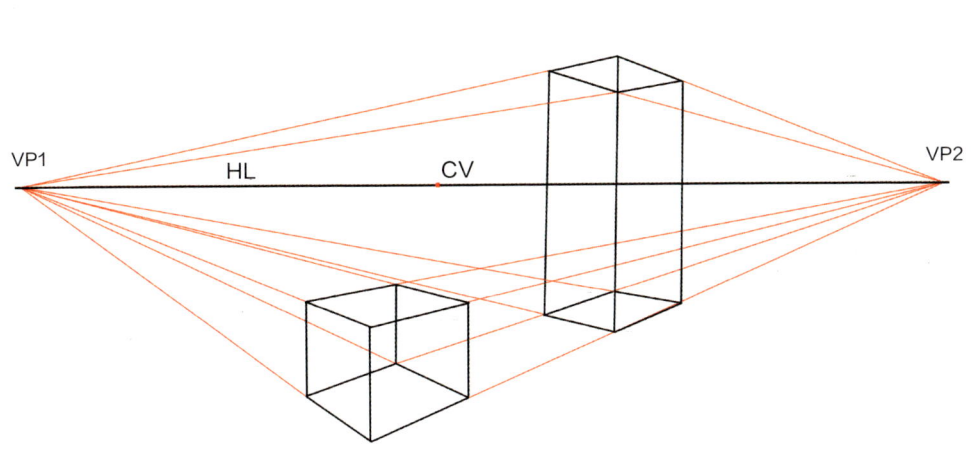

Fig.2.9 Diagram representation of two-point perspective

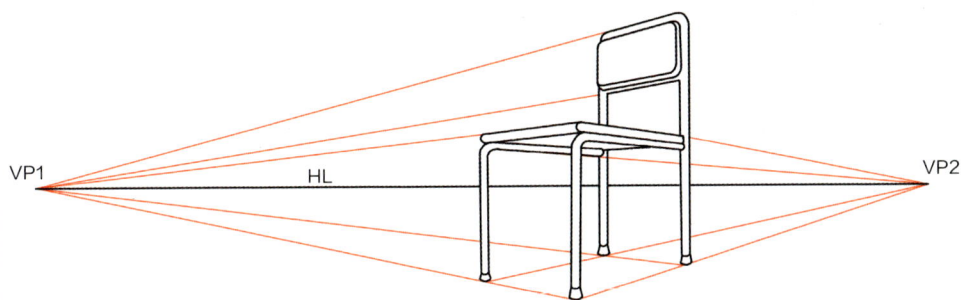

Fig.2.10 Two-point perspective analysis of a chair

Two-point perspective

Two-point perspective is also known as angular perspective. Take a cube as an example. When the left and the right sides of cube form a certain angle with the image plane, the extension of lines of the sides converge at two vanishing points, hence it is called two-point perspective, as shown in Fig.2.7 to Fig.2.10. In two-point perspective, the observer looks at the object from the turning plane instead of the front. The picture rendered by two-point perspective can reflect the depth more realistically, but it can be difficult for beginners to master as it is easily prone to distortion.

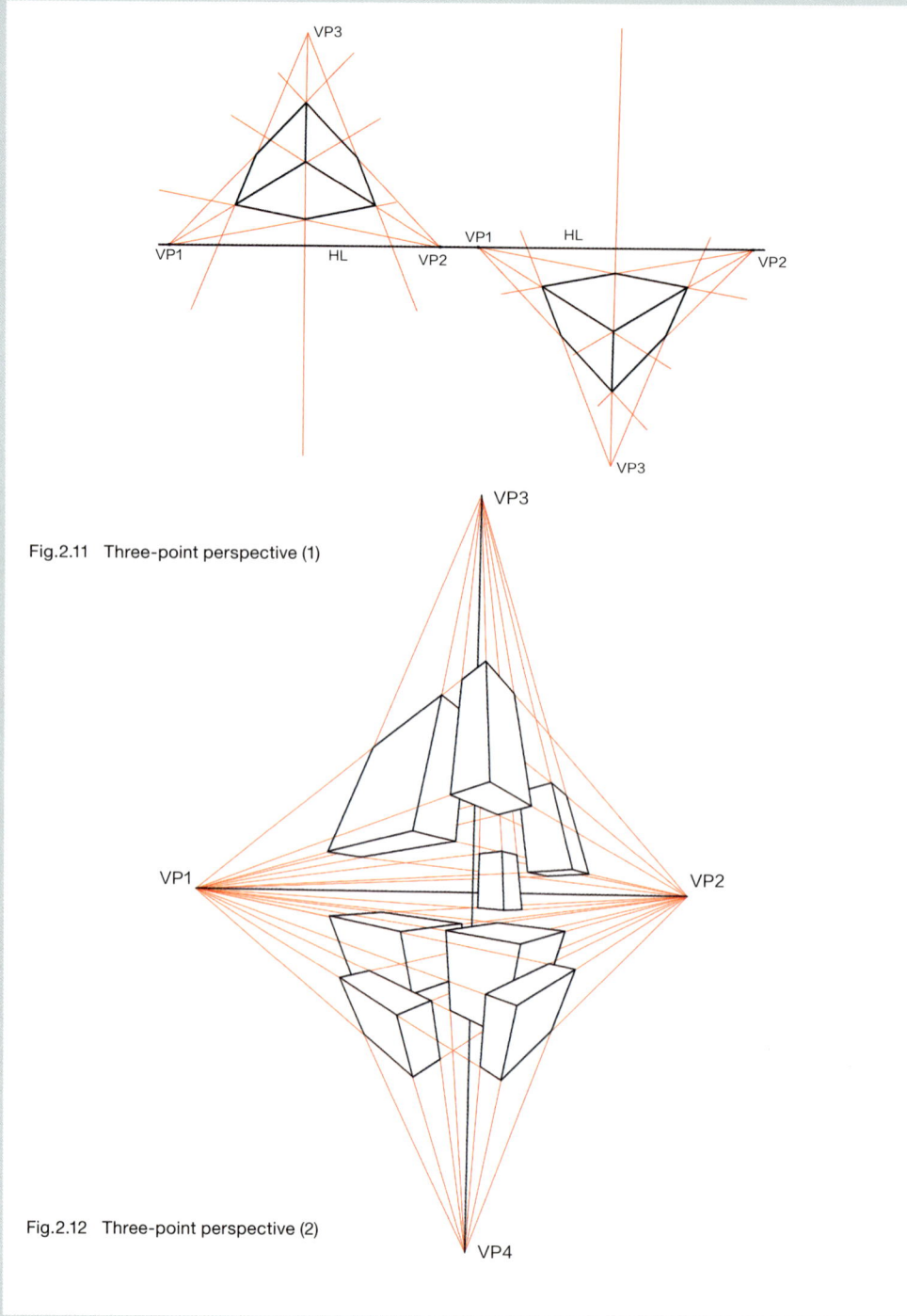

Fig.2.11　Three-point perspective (1)

Fig.2.12　Three-point perspective (2)

Three-point perspective

Three-point perspective is also known as oblique perspective. Take a cube as an example. When all the sides or edges of the cube are not parallel to the image plane, extensions of three sides converge at three vanishing points. This is called three-point perspective. In addition to the two vanishing points from the earlier two-point perspective, the three-point perspective has an additional vanishing point. Therefore, the cube is relatively tilted in comparison to the image plane. The third vanishing point, above or below the horizon line, represents a perspective expression of the height. Usually, it expresses the sight angle of a tall object seen from above or below, as shown in Fig.2.11 to Fig.2.13.

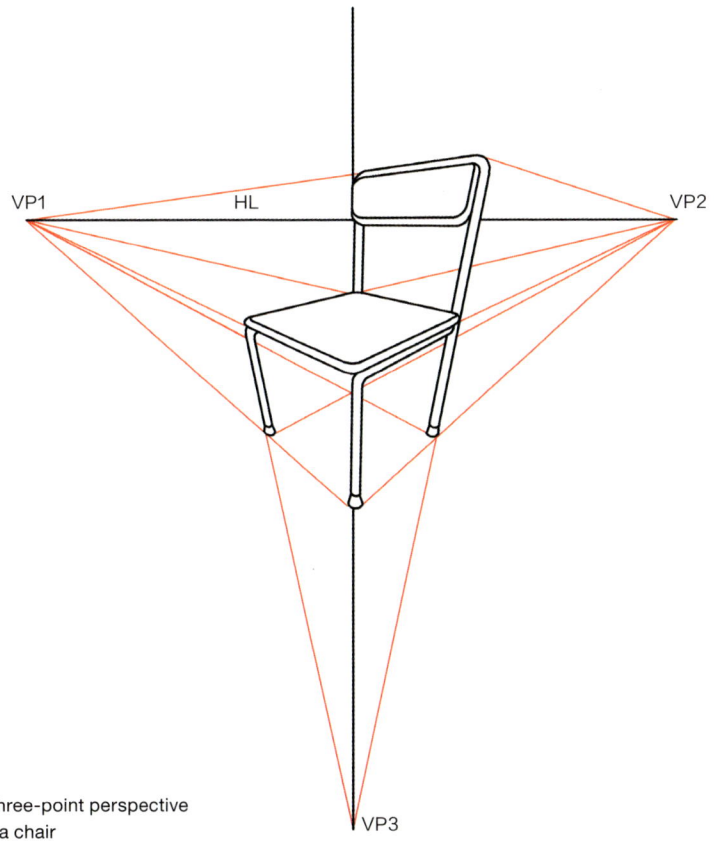

Fig.2.13 Three-point perspective analysis of a chair

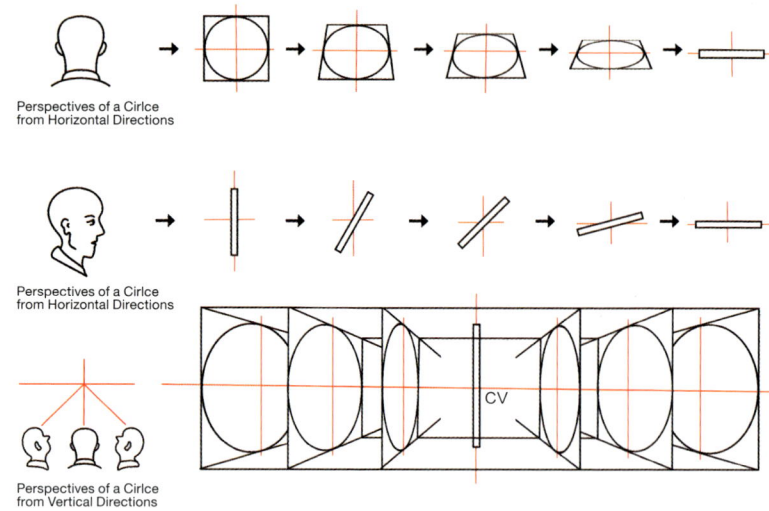

Fig.2.14 Principles of circle in perspective

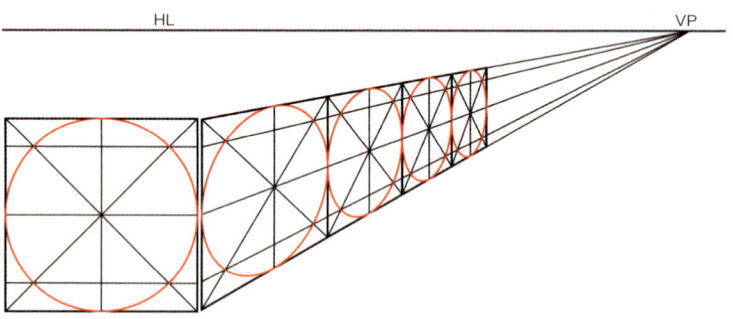

Fig.2.15 Circle in one-point perspective (1)

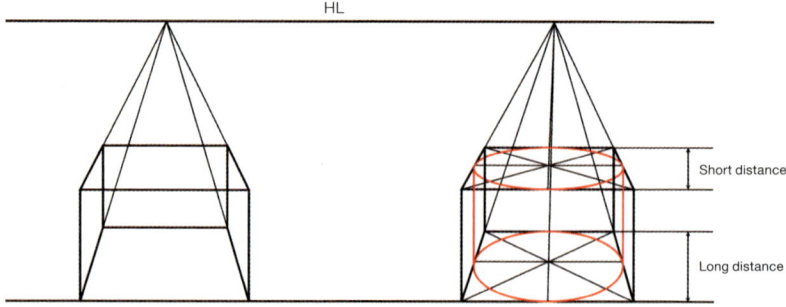

Fig.2.16 Circle in one-point perspective (2)

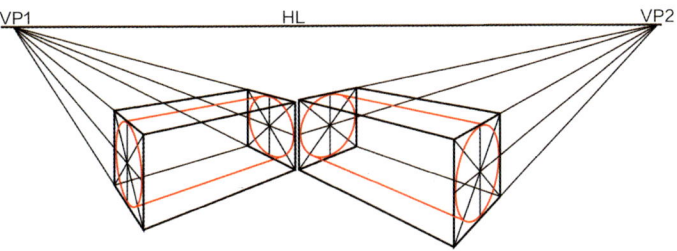

Fig.2.17 Circle in two-point perspective

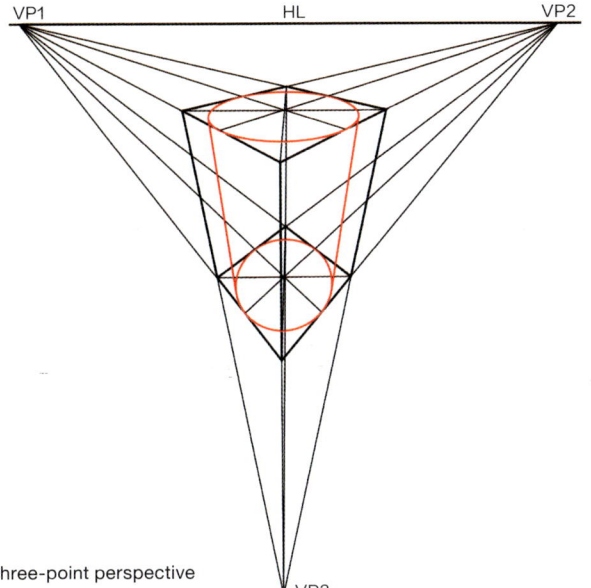

Fig.2.18 Circle in three-point perspective

Perspective of a circle

The ellipse and circle are shapes that are common in product expression techniques. Generally, the perspective of a circle that is parallel to the plane is a perfect circle, but the circle that is perpendicular to the plane gradually changes to an ellipse due to the foreshortening effects. The shape of the ellipse is related to distance—a more distant semicircle looks smaller than another that is closer. Curves in the perspective of a cirlce should be even and natural, especially at both ends. Corresponding perspective techniques are shown in Fig.2.14 to Fig.2.18.

Factors Influencing Perspective

Position

The position at which the object is placed directly influences the perspective of the object in the image plane. You can adjust the perspective position by changing the object's position based on the requirements of the image plane. Usually, 30°, 45°, and 60° are used. The relationships among the object, plane, and sight angle directly affect product perspective image on the plane, as it directly impacts the main features, scale, and size of the product, and the visual image of the design graphics, as shown in Fig.2.19.

Perspective positions can have a great impact on design rendering, so designers should should carefully choose this aspect. Relatively natural effects (that is similar to what the naked eye sees) may be seen using certain perspective positions when drawing products, while other positions may bring an opposite result. Moreover, an object can be shown to be larger or smaller. The perspective position is crucial in creating a favorable impression of the product.

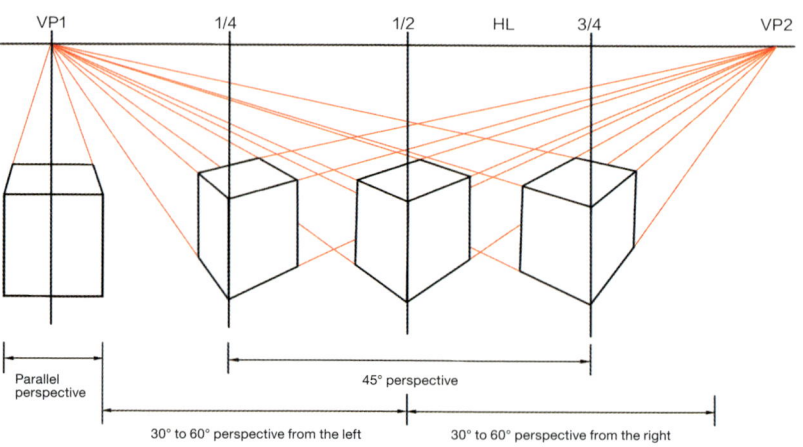

Fig.2.19 Analysis of various positions in perspective

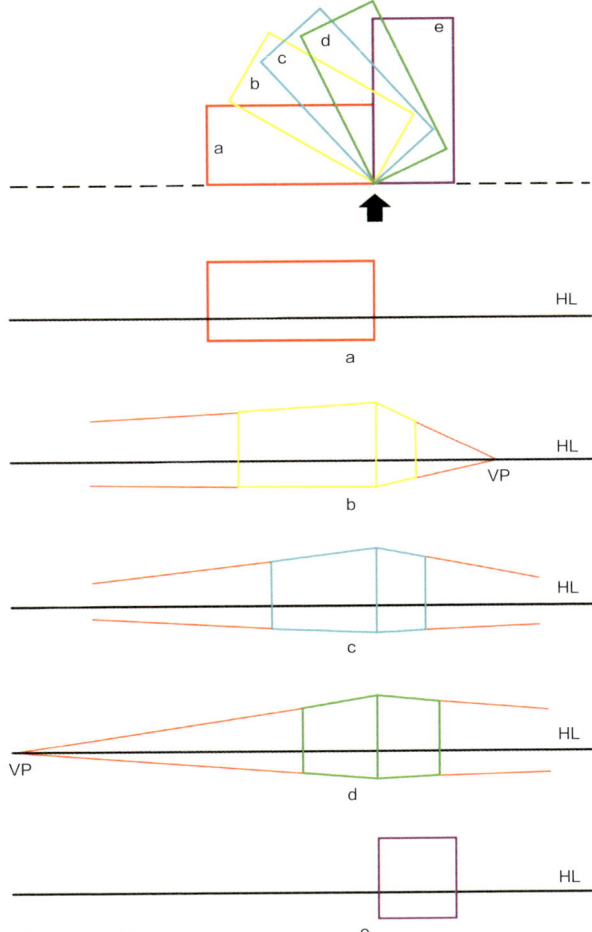

Fig.2.20　Analysis of various angles in perspective

Angle

A one-point perspective is created when the angle between the front of the object and the picture plane is 0°, and the front appears to be flat. When the angle is greater than 0° and less than 90°, and there is an angle between the front and the plane, it is a two-point perspective; when the front is perpendicular to the plane and the side is parallel to the plane, a one-point perspectiveis created. These are shown in Fig.2.20.

Analyzing the perspective angle facilitates the understanding of object modeling characteristics and creation of the entire modeling.

Visual distance

According to perspective principles, the greater the visual distance, the farther is the vanishing point. Accordingly, the perspective of the object is correspondingly flatter, and the front, and the side face are more unfolded; otherwise, they look steeper and smaller. If the visual distance is too short, the perspective we get might be unclear. On the contrary, the perspective obtained is too minute to detail and it becomes hard to represent the spatial and three-dimensional sense if the visual distance is too long. The object distance, hence, must be intermediate, as shown in Fig.2.21.

Height of horizon line

The height of the horizon line can affect the product's perspective image. An object placed higher than the horizon line looks taller and bigger. For instance, this makes the object look much bigger, as in outdoor buildings and large machines. When the center of the object and the horizon line overlap, the perspective of the object is flatter, and the object appears stable but tends to be monotonous. When the object is below the horizon line, the image shows a top-down effect, showing more faces and various changes in the image. Therefore, the choice of the height of horizon line should be based on the expression requirements of the object, that is, the size and bulk of the object that is required to be projected, as shown in Fig.2.22.

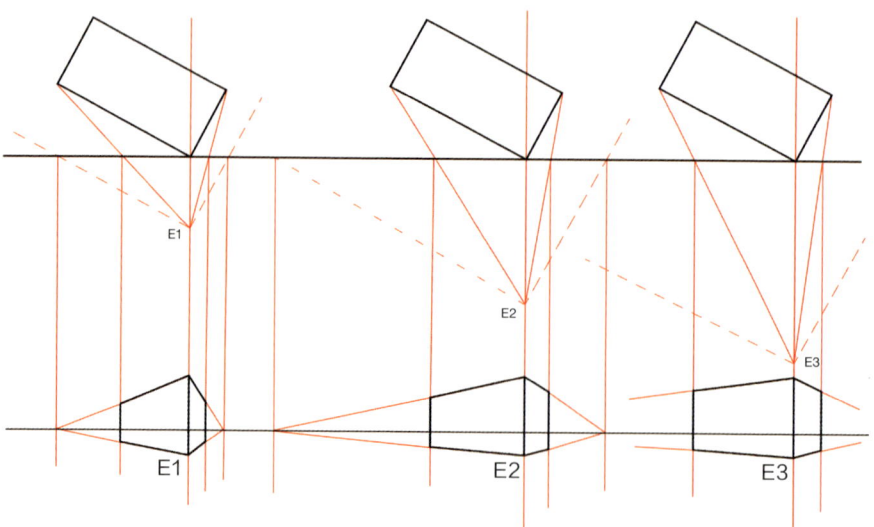

Fig.2.21 Analysis of visual distance

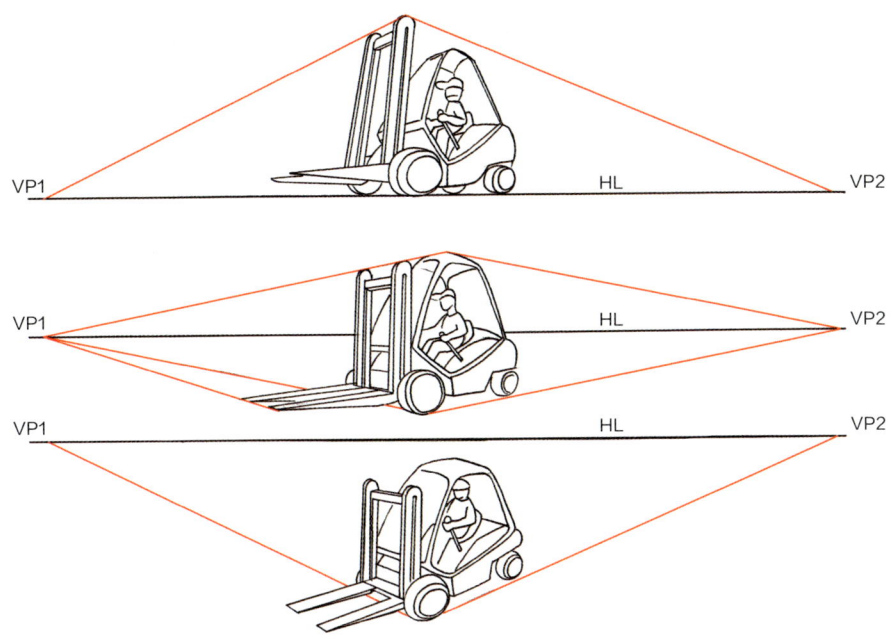

Fig.2.22 Analysis of the height of horizon line

Composition

Composition refers to the combination, as an organic whole, of various aspects of the image, such as layout, shape, proportion, space, color, volume, line, in a certain way on a limited plane space, that most effectively communicates the required content, emotion and thought. To define a composition, firstly you need to picture the size and shape. Secondly, in the limited frame, the visual images are structurally arranged to highlight the theme. The form and shape factors are used to make the picture diversified, organized, harmonious, and unified to attract the viewer's attention to the representation at the center of the plane. Metaphorically speaking, the composition of a picture is like shooting a movie, in which each scene is a picture, and each picture involves a composition. Nevertheless, perspective and composition are complementary, and so are their features and challenges. The composition of product modeling aims to showcase the product characteristics in the best manner.

Fig.2.23 Tools for hand drawing

Tools

As the saying goes, "A craftsman is only as good as his tools." To create good hand renderings, you require the right tools and materials. Thus, every designer needs to find the right methods to express their designs, and they must conform to the trends and real needs of the society, as shown in Fig.2.23.

Design sketches and final renderings are the two basic methods of displaying creativity in product design. The tools and paper are the main media for expressing the image, and these are indispensable for any hand-drawing form. Proficiency in pen and paper is the key to drawing good design sketches and effective final renderings.

Product design tools and materials available for hand drawing are diverse. These include pencils, pens, ballpoint pens, and needle pens for drawing lines, markers, and pastels for coloring, as well as ancillary tools such as correction pens, highlighters, rulers, French curves, and so on.

Pencils

There are two types of pencils—monochrome pencils and colored pencils. Monochrome pencils include sketching pencils and hand-drawing pencils. There is a wide range of sketching pencils that is available, as shown

Fig.2.24 Sketching pencils

Fig.2.25 Hand drawing pencils

Fig.2.26 Water-soluble colored pencils

Fig.2.27 Water-insoluble colored pencils

in Fig.2.24 and Fig.2.25. Soft lead pencils are easy to use and help achieve a rich shading effect of black, white, and gray due to the soft lead, sensitiveness to the hardness of the paper, and the pressure of drawing. The hard lead of hand-drawing pencils make it easier to draw an even line of moderate shading. We can choose the type of pencil for drawing based on personal preference.

Colored pencils fall into two main types—water-soluble and water-insoluble, as shown in Fig.2.26 and Fig.2.27. Generally, water-soluble colored pencils contain less wax, are of delicate texture, and similar to pastels in brightness, so they are easy to color but less transparent. The main feature of water-soluble colored pencils is that the color is water soluble. After applying the color with the pencil, we can create rich layers of overlapping colors similar to watercolor effects by coloring over it with a brush dipped in water. However, it can be challenging for beginners to use and they are expensive.

Water-insoluble colored pencils, are not soluble in water. They resemble crayons, containing more wax, are delicate in texture and the color is lighter than that of water-soluble colored pencils. The high transparency of water-insoluble colored pencils makes it easier to overlap colors. This feature and its inexpensive price make it an ideal tool for beginners to practise color overlay techniques.

Fig.2.28 Pens

Fig.2.29 Ballpoint pens

Pens, ballpoint pens & technical pens

As shown in Fig.2.28, pens are used to produce lines of varying thickness. These can effectively present the outline, spatial hierarchy, changes in light and shadow, and material texture of the product and its background. The disadvantages are that the amount of ink is not easy to control, and the maintenance costs are high.

Ballpoint pens offer uniform inking, fine lines, rich layers, and are available in varying sizes, making them more suitable for detailing than pens, as shown in Fig.2.29. In addition, the ballpoint pen is easy to use and affordable. However, since it's not easy to rectify errors, you are expected to finish drawing in only one stroke with ballpoint pen, and this requires long-term practise.

Compared to ballpoint pens, technical pens produce more even lines, which are finer and look neater. The technical pen, shown in Fig.2.30 and Fig.2.31, has a fountain-pen body with a nib that is a hollow steel ring of about 2 cm with a movable thin steel needle inside. Shaking the technical pen up and down periodically can dislodge any paper fibers blocking the pen nip. When drawing with a technical pen, we can make relatively precise lines of constant width. The size of the nib determines the line width. The nib

Fig.2.30 Technical drawing pens

Fig.2.31 Technical drawing pens with various nib sizes

thickness can vary from 0.1 mm to 1.2 mm and they dispense ink evenly and smoothly. Designers use 3 different types of technical pens—the fine, the medium, and the broad-nibbed technical pens.

Marker pens

The marker pen or the marker, shown in Fig.2.32, was developed for hand-drawing renderings, and is often used to quickly draw design ideas, as well as design renderings. Markers are popular as they are available in rich colors, simple to use, help in quickly creating drawing, and are easy to carry. They are preferred by designers due to their incomparable performance in hand drawing.

There are various types of markers, including water-based, oil-based, alcohol-based, single-headed, double-headed, extra-wide, disposable and refillable pens. Markers are also available in gray and colored series, and each pen has a color number. As long as the brand numbers are the same, the color of the markers is identical.

Colors of water-based markers are vibrant and transparent, yet repeated color overlaying could turn colors into gray and tear the paper easily. Water-based markers are generally disposable, cheap, odorless, and environmentally friendly, so they are suitable for children.

Oil-based markers, shown in Fig.2.33, also known as marker pens, have soft nibs. They

Fig.2.32　Water-based marker pens

have transparency, provide good coverage, and are quick drying and water resistant. They can keep the paper intact even after repeatedly drawing on the paper, and offer a more seamless connection between each stroke.

Inks of alcohol-based markers shown in Fig.2.34 and Fig.2.35 featuring transparent colors, are quick-drying and water resistant, enable free color mixing, dry faster and are non-toxic. You can alternate pen nibs in line with different needs as most of the pens are double-tipped and can be refilled with ink. These markers are widely accepted among design students and design professionals, but they are expensive.

Correction pens & highlighters

In product freehand rendering, correction pens and highlighters, shown in Fig.2.36 and Fig.2.37, are mainly used for the final decoration and adjustment of the picture, which can enhance the products' light effect and texture, highlighting the crucial features. Similar to the correction fluid, correction pens are suitable for whitening a larger area

Fig.2.33   Oil-based marker pens

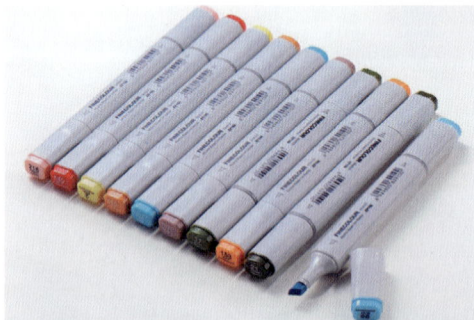

Fig.2.34   Alcohol-based marker pens

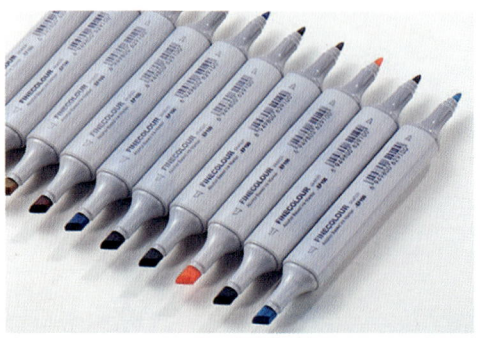

Fig.2.35   Alcohol-based marker pens of various colors

Fig.2.36   Highlighters

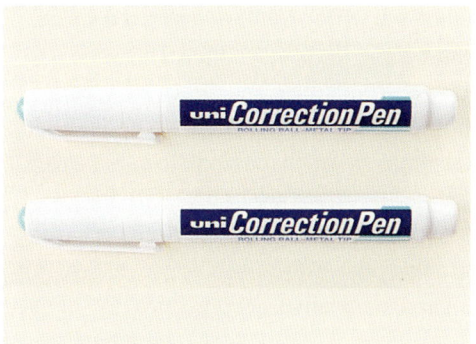

Fig.2.37 Correction pens

Fig.2.38 Pastels

due to more ink output, good coverage, and relatively thick layer. Compared with the correction pen, it is easier to control the amount of ink output and the line width with a highlighter, so it can more finely and professionally modify image details.

Pastels

Pastels shown in Fig.2.38, are a sort of powdered pigment, and mainly used to color products design images, like a marker. The color of the pastel is more uniform and natural than that of the marker. Pastels can be used to color large areas, give soft gradient effects and are suitable for creating effects of highly reflective materials such as curved surfaces, metals, and glass used in products. Additionally, there are pastels of many colors available for color modulation. Care must be taken not to apply too much of the pastel as it might stain the picture or blur it.

Rulers, compasses & French curves

Tools such as rulers and compasses assist in drawing neat and precise product renderings. As shown in Fig.2.39 to Fig.2.42, rulers fall into straight edges, flat splines, French curves, elliptical guides, circle plates, to name a few.

Flat spline, also known as flexible curve, is a kind of double-sided measuring tape with a flexible metal core encased in rubber

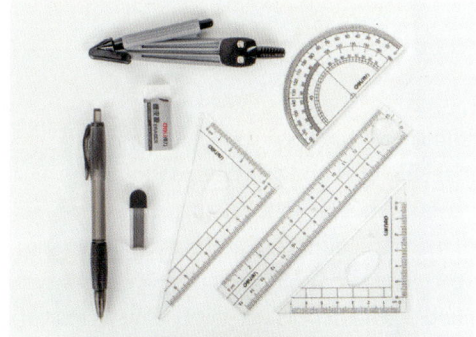

Fig.2.39 Rulers and compasses

Preparation for Perspective, Principle of Composition and Tools   037

Fig.2.40 Flat spline

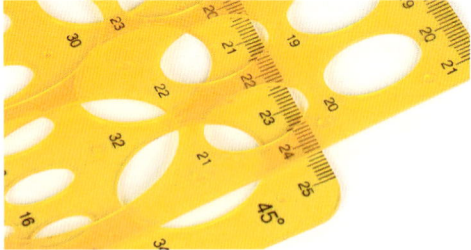

Fig.2.41 Elliptical guides

Fig.2.42 French curves

with scales the curved edges. They can measure arcs and can be used to draw various arc shapes and free curves because of their high curvature and snake-like shape. To draw a curve with the flat spline, firstly you should predetermine several points, secondly connect the different points by twisting the strip, and while slightly pressing the spline, draw along the spline edges. This way, you can get your curve. The disadvantages of the spline lie in its low accuracy and uneven distribution, which may lead to some errors.

French curve, a kind of cloud-shaped ruler, is a thin plate with curved edges, either internal or external, used to draw non-circular free curves of varying radii. These cannot, however, measure a curve and have a fixed curvature.

Paper

There are many types of paper for hand drawing, including drawing paper, marker paper, colored cardboard, copy paper, and so on, as shown in Fig.2.43 to Fig.2.46.

Renderings use drawing paper of moderate thickness and good ink permeability, which are relatively inexpensive and can bear multiple repeated pen strokes.

Marker paper, shown in Fig.2.44, specially developed for marker renderings, is delicate, white, impermeable to ink, and has strong adhesion to toner, but it is relatively expensive.

Colored cardboard, shown in Fig.2.45, is generally thick and comes in a wide range of colors. When using colored cardboard, paper color is usually taken as the mid-tone, the dark part is deepened and the bright part is whitened, which can make the picture color harmonious and uniform, and then used to produce the unique effect. It is difficult to control the color and grayscale, which requires repeated trials in practise.

Copy paper, shown in Fig.2.46, such as modern office paper is available everywhere. Its texture is whiter and is available in various thicknesses. Its cheap price and uniform size make it easier to bind and store. It is an ideal choice for beginners to practise sketching and to train on hand-painting training.

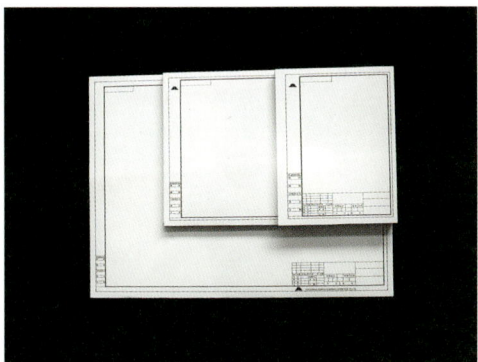

Fig.2.43　Drawing paper

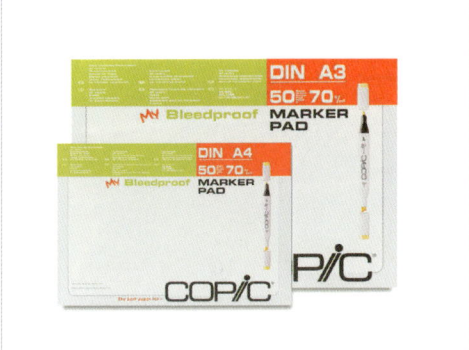

Fig.2.44　Marker paper

Fig.2.45　Colored cardboard

Fig.2.46　Copy paper

Preparation for Perspective, Principle of Composition and Tools　　**039**

Basics of Expression Techniques

CHAPTER 3

The basic skills of expression techniques include those of line-painting, modeling designs and marker pens. The purpose of practising the basics of expression techniques is to improve the brain-eye-hand coordination so that, with the control of the brain, the hands can accurately draw out the picture in the mind. This requires the proficiency in lines and modeling. Training in techniques starts from the basics and requires the grasp of basic methods and techniques as well as plenty of practise. High buildings rise from the flat ground and a higher building requires a firm foundation.

Basic Skills of Line-Painting

Being the most basic hand-drawing element, lines are classified into straight lines and curves.

Straight line

Straight lines include horizontal lines, vertical lines, and oblique lines. Straight lines are frequently used for hand drawing of products and serve as edges, centerlines, or perspective lines. Also, straight lines are mostly used for sketching and summarizing structures. There are three straight line types—bold in the middle and thin at both ends, bold at one end and thin at the other, and having the same weight at both ends.

How to practise drawing the first type of line—bold in the middle and thin at both ends:

Mark two points on the paper at random (the distance between the two points should be 10—15cm), and then quickly connect the two points with the tip of the pen. As practise before drawing the line, you can trace a straight line back and forth between the two points in the air with the pen tip. Once you are confident of the line, quickly draw through both points to get a straight line, as shown in Fig.3.1.

How to practise drawing the second type of line—bold at one end and thin at the other:

Randomly mark two dots (the distance between them should be 10—15cm), place the tip of the pen on the starting point, quickly draw towards the end point, and leave the paper just right before the pen tip reaches the end point, as shown in Fig.3.2.

How to practise drawing the third type of line—having the same weight at both ends:

Mark two points anywhere on the paper (the distance between them should be 10—15cm), place the tip of the pen on the starting point and quickly draw through to the end point, then lift the pen tip off the paper, as shown in Fig.3.3.

It's a basic requirement in product freehand drawing to be skillful at drawing straight lines. This can be achieved by using fixed lines, points or a direction.

How do we draw a straight line using fixed lines? Draw two parallel lines, either horizontal or vertical, and then draw freehand straight lines within these two parallel lines. Ensure that you keep the straight lines as parallel and as straight as you can, as shown in Fig.3.4. Tips: first, hold the pen or pencil with your natural grip and not too tight; second, move the pen smoothly and quickly; third, pay attention to the starting and end points of the stroke.

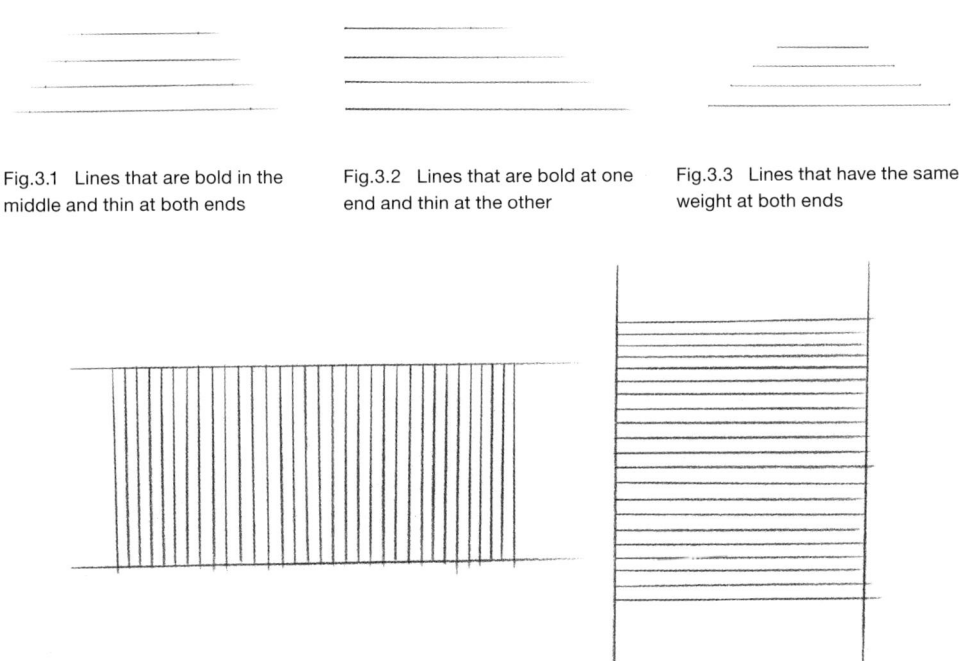

Fig.3.1 Lines that are bold in the middle and thin at both ends

Fig.3.2 Lines that are bold at one end and thin at the other

Fig.3.3 Lines that have the same weight at both ends

Fig.3.4 Drawing straight lines using fixed lines

Basics of Expression Techniques

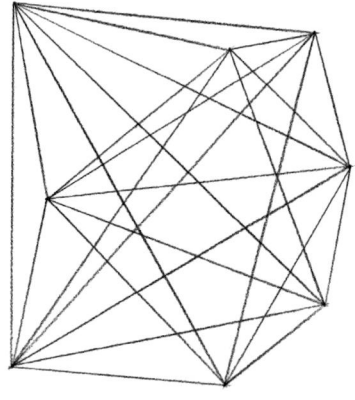 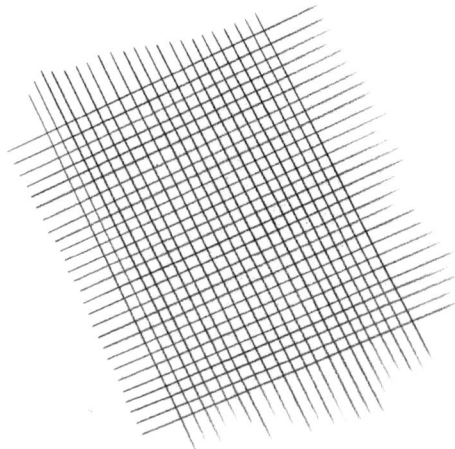

Fig.3.5 Drawing straight lines using fixed points

Fig.3.6 Drawing straight lines in a fixed direction

How do we draw a straight line using fixed points? Set some points wherever you like on a paper, connect them with a straight line, making the end point of each straight line coincide with a given point as shown in Fig.3.5. Tips: first, make sure the points are scattered but aligned; second, adjust the angle of your wrist when you draw to connect two points; third, pay attention to the pressure you apply and the smoothness while holding the pen.

How do we draw a straight line using a fixed direction? Set an oblique direction, make parallel lines in this direction, and then crisscross these lines, as shown in Fig.3.6. Tip: Control the line spacing and keep lines parallel and steady.

When practising drawing straight lines, sit straight in a relaxed posture. Draw fast, but accurately with consistent force. Adjust the angle of your wrist as much as possible. Keep the gaps between lines as small and as uniform as possible. Draw the line as straight as possible in the required direction.

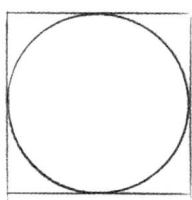

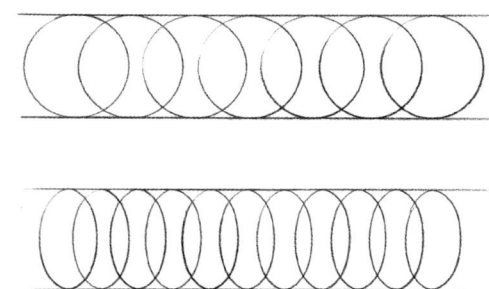

Fig.3.7 Drawing circles by setting four tangents

Fig.3.8 Drawing circles or ellipses by setting two tangents

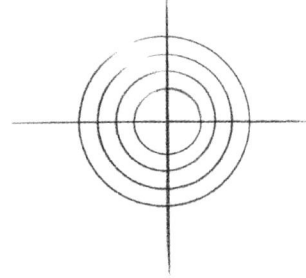

Fig.3.9 Drawing circles by setting a center

Fig.3.10 Drawing ellipses by setting a point of tangency

Curve

Curves include circles (perfectly round curves), ellipse curves, and irregular curves. Curves play an essential part in hand drawing when it comes to product design due to their common use in soft and transitional curving effects. In addition, curves are more often used to show buttons and fillet in detail.

When practising drawing circles and ellipses, there are five techniques—set a tangent, a center, a point of tangency, arcs, or a cambered surface.

How do we draw circles or ellipses using fixed tangents? Draw a perfectly circular curve within the four edges of the parallelogram and make it tangent to the edges, as shown in Fig.3.7. Another method is to draw two parallel lines and a circle or ellipse curve tangent to them, as shown in Fig.3.8.

How do we draw circles and ellipses by setting a center? As shown in Fig.3.9, first, determine a center with a vertical axis; second, draw perfectly circular curves that are evenly spaced from small to large.

Basics of Expression Techniques   045

How do we draw circles and ellipses by setting a point of tangency? As shown in Fig.3.10, firstly draw a big perfect circle or a big ellipse curve; secondly pick any point as the point of tangency from the curve, and then draw another smaller circle or ellipse inward evenly that passes through the first curve.

How do we draw circles and ellipses by setting arcs? First, set lines with two arcs that are bell-shaped; second, draw an ellipse curve tangent to and between these two arcs, as shown in Fig.3.11. Pay attention to the perspective.

How do we draw ellipses by setting a cambered surface? Known as progressive elliptical, a cambered surface is a gradual arrangement with curving effects, which show distance, size, and perspective. When drawing, pay attention to the variation of its perspective vanishing point, as shown in Fig.3.12 to Fig.3.14.

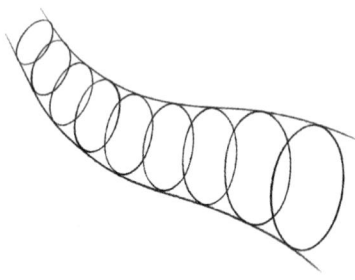

Fig.3.11 Drawing ellipses by setting arcs

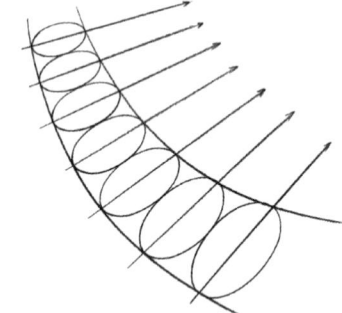

Fig.3.12 Drawing ellipses by setting a cambered surface (1)

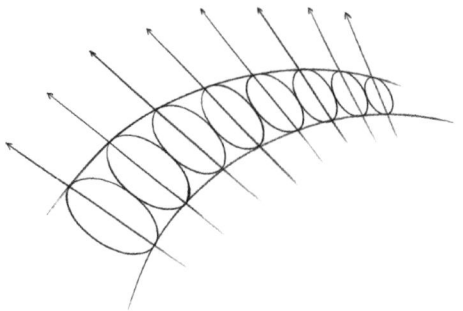

Fig.3.13 Drawing ellipses by setting a cambered surface (2)

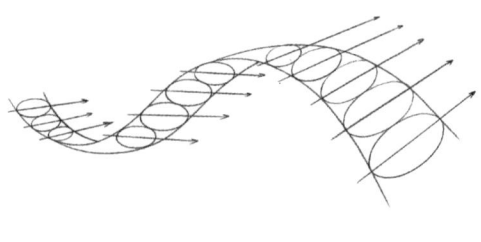

Fig.3.14 Drawing ellipses by setting a cambered surface (3)

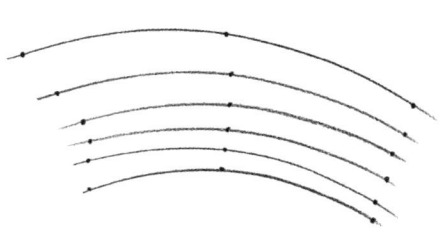

Fig.3.15 Defining a line with three points

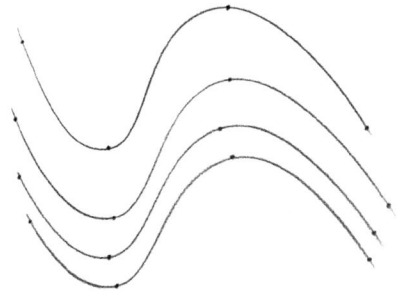

Fig.3.16 Defining a line with four points

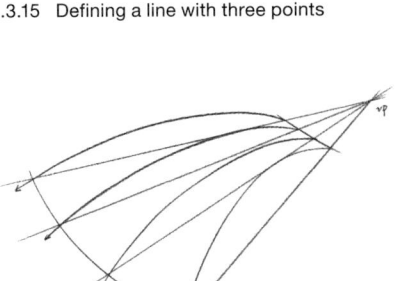

Fig.3.17 Defining a line by perspective (1)

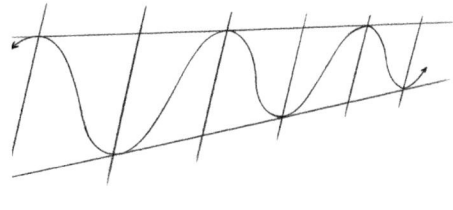

Fig.3.18 Defining a line by perspective (2)

There are three ways to practise irregular curves. First, define a line with three points; second, define a line with four points; third, define a line by perspective. While practising, hands should be as relaxed as possible, the pen/pencil should be perpendicular to the paper, and move the pen/pencil tip in the air to practise the right curve track and pass through a few points. The specific steps are as follows.

Define a line with three points: As shown in Fig.3.15, set three dots that are not in a straight line and then draw any curve to go through these three points.

Define a line with four points: As shown in Fig.3.16, make four dots that are not in a straight line and then plot any curve that goes through these four points.

Define a line by perspective: As shown in Fig.3.17 and Fig.3.18, draw perspective lines. Then draw regular curves according to perspective lines. Try to draw using swift stokes and pay attention to perspective.

Basics of Modeling Design

Today, we find diverse products in the market in various shapes. Given this diversity and complexity of products, we can analyze the characteristics of models in terms of product design. The first step is to simplify these models and turn them into geometry so that you can understand the essential of these models. They are common geometric shapes—square, rectangle, trapezoid, circle, ellipse, cylinder, isosceles triangle, scalene triangle and etc.

For most products, their models can be considered as the variants and derivatives of basic geometric solids, which are generally modified according to a certain principles of basic geometric solids. Therefore, when designing a product, it is necessary to do an in-depth analysis of the product model by breaking down its structure and assembling the elements to recreate the product model.

To develop the basic skills of modeling design, you need to be familiar with five aspects, namely basic geometric solids, geometric combinations, geometric chamfers, geometric fillets, and geometric surfaces.

Basic geometric solids

Basic geometric solids include cubes, spheres, spheroids, cylinders, cones, prismatoids, rings, tubes, elbow pipes, etc. The practise of basic geometric solids is a process of analysis by straight lines and curves, according to perspective changes and internal structural lines, as shown in Fig.3.19 to Fig.3.26.

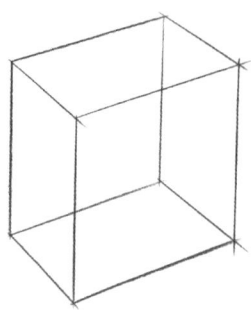

Fig.3.19 Cube

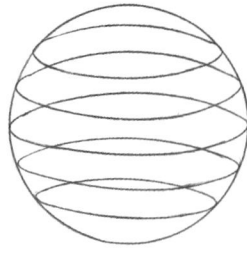

Fig.3.20 Sphere

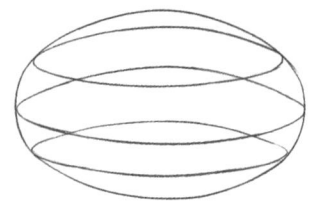

Fig.3.21 Spheroid

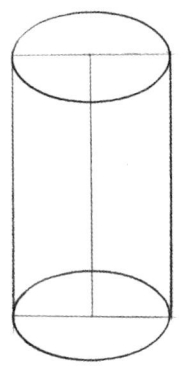

Fig.3.22 Circular cylinder

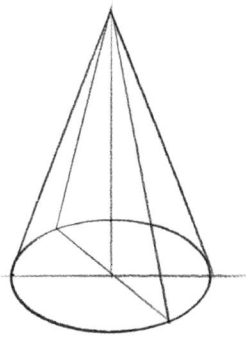

Fig.3.23 Cone

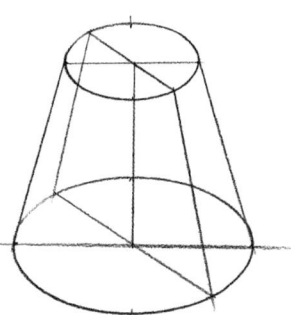

Fig.3.24 Prismatoid

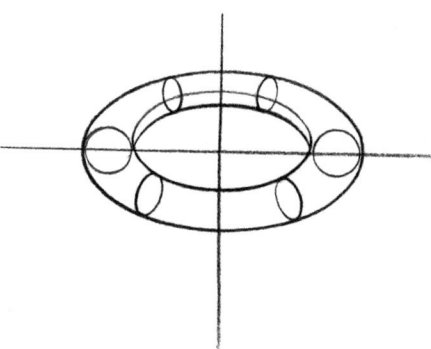

Fig.3.25 Ring

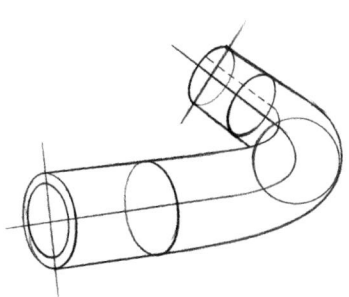

Fig.3.26 Tube and elbow pipe

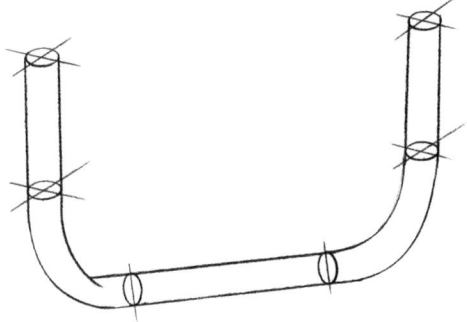

Basics of Expression Techniques **049**

Geometric combinations

Geometric combinations can be divided into geometric combinations of one kind and geometric combinations of different kinds. Addition and subtraction are adopted in shape variation of geometric combination exercises, such as scooping a sphere from a cube or looping a cylinder. Basically, while practising drawing geometric combinations, straight lines should be combined with curves, bump changes should be made, structures should be well-proportioned, as shown in Fig.3.27 to Fig.3.29.

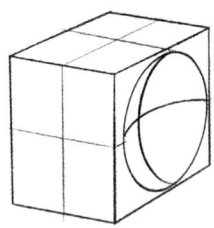
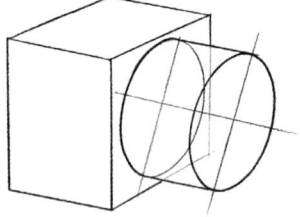

Fig.3.27 A combination of geometric solid shapes (1)

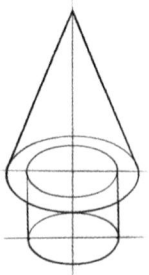
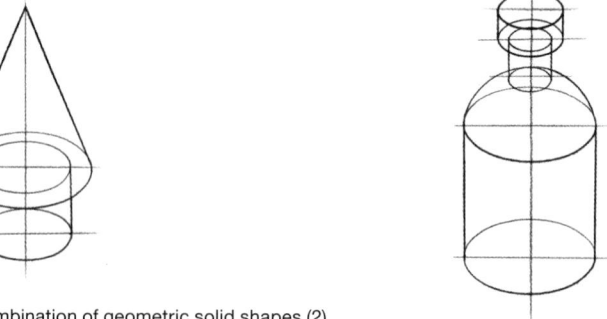

Fig.3.28 A combination of geometric solid shapes (2)

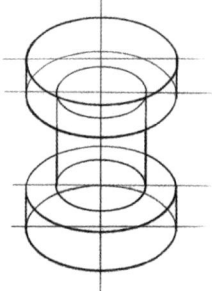
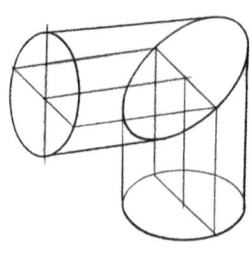

Fig.3.29 A combination of geometric solid shapes (3)

Geometric chamfers

Make a cut along a 90° edge so that it slopes, resulting in a 45° chamfer, formed by the small plane and the main body of the geometric solids. The chamfer angle depends on the design needs of the product itself and needs not necessarily be exactly 45°. When practising, initially, you can draw geometric solids, fix points according to the perspective principles, and finally chamfer the geometry with lines, as shown in Fig.3.30 to Fig.3.33.

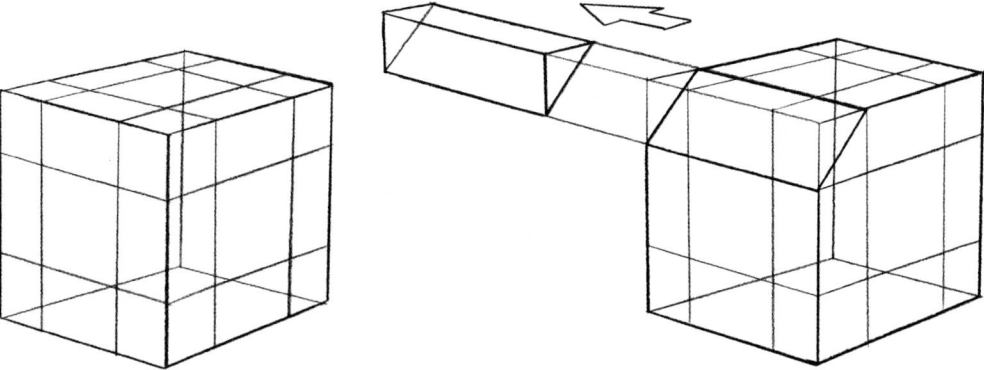

Fig.3.30 Geometric chamfer (1)

Fig.3.31 Geometric chamfer (2)

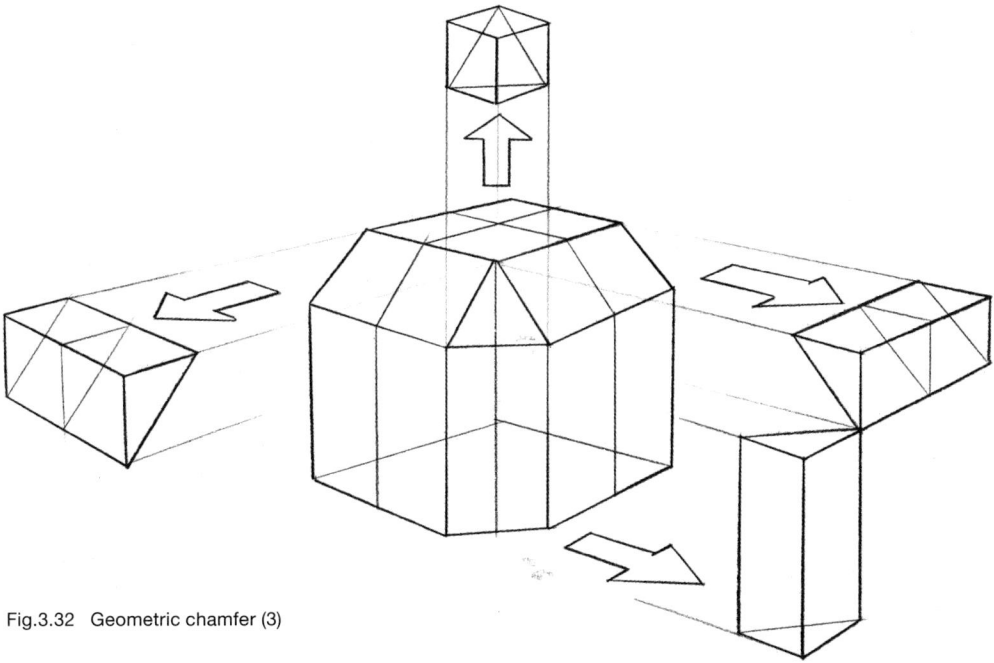

Fig.3.32 Geometric chamfer (3)

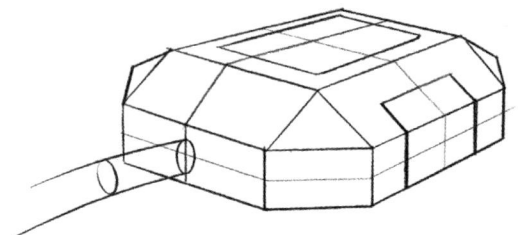

Fig.3.33 Chamfers in product design

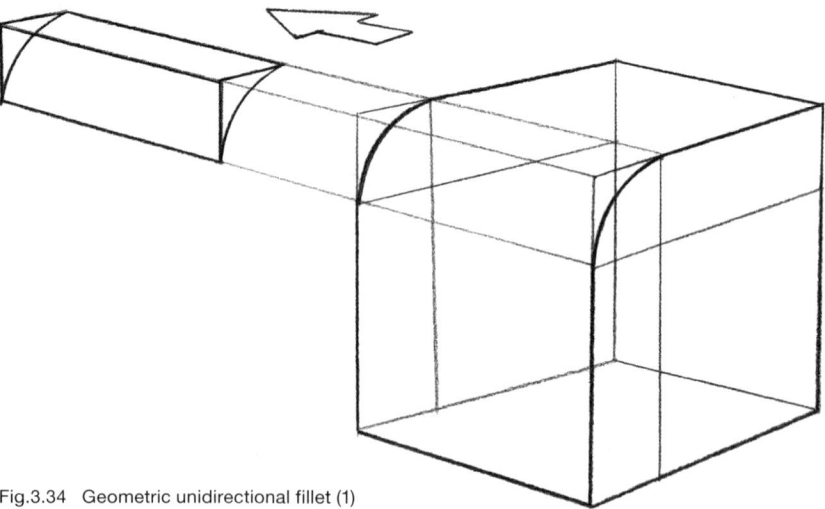

Fig.3.34 Geometric unidirectional fillet (1)

Geometric fillets

Fillet is gained by replacing the original corner with a circular arc tangent at both of its ends. The radius of the arc limits the size of the fillet. A geometric fillet could be a unidirectional fillet or composite fillet.

The unidirectional fillet has an edge that is processed to be cylinder-like in one perspective direction. Composite fillets have several edges that are processed to be circle-like in two perspective directions, as shown in Fig.3.34 to Fig.3.37.

Most products have fillets for aesthetics, user-friendliness, and safety and don't affect the internal space, they are present structurally for the convenience of using grinding tools and for manufacturing processes, as shown in Fig.3.38 to Fig.3.41.

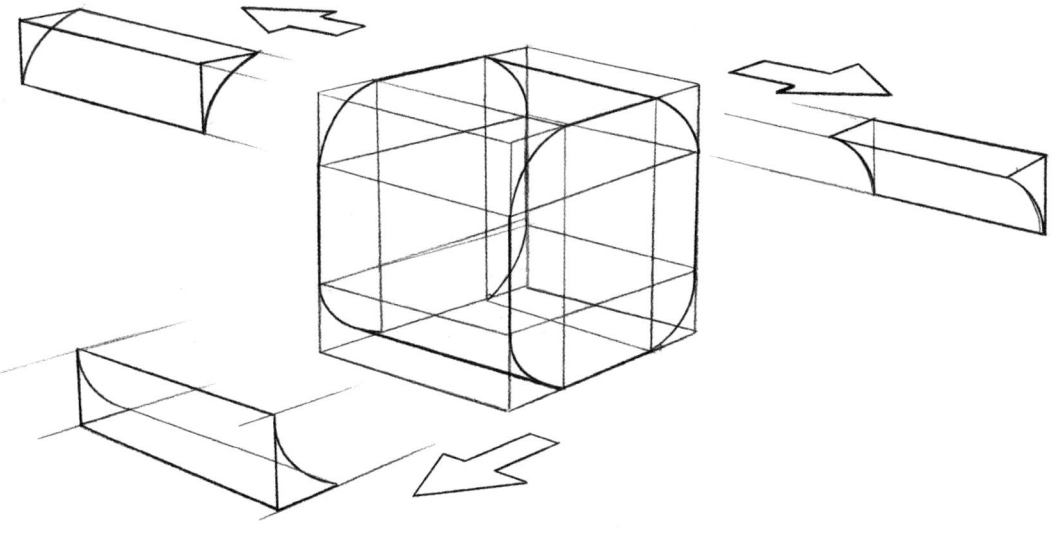

Fig.3.35 Geometric unidirectional fillet (2)

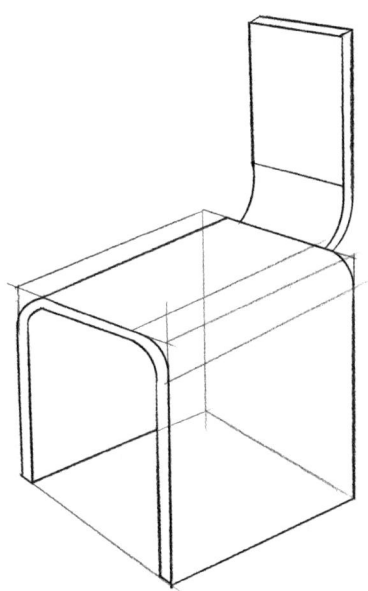

Fig.3.36 Unidirectional fillet design in a product (1)

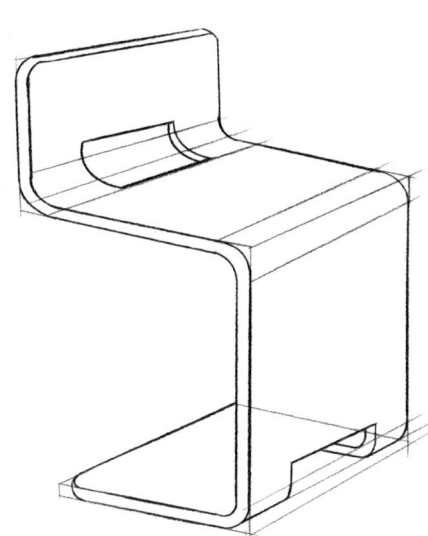

Fig.3.37 Unidirectional fillet design in a product (2)

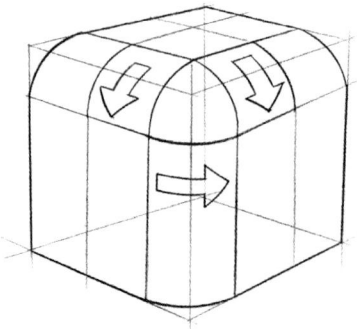
Fig.3.38　Geometric composite fillets (1)

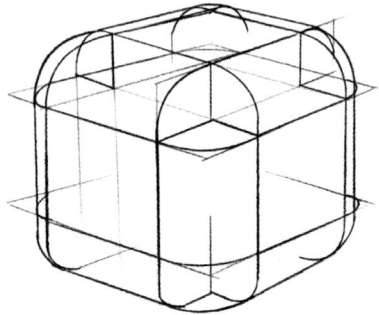
Fig.3.39　Geometric composite fillets (2)

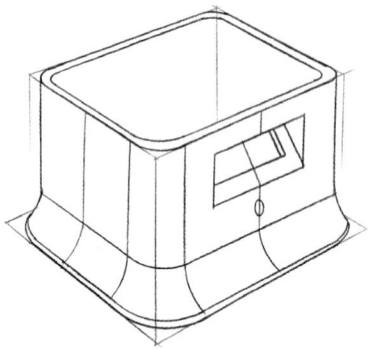
Fig.3.40　Composite fillet design (1)

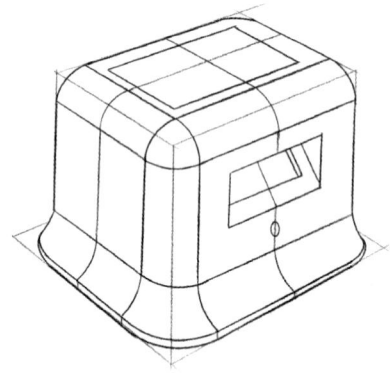
Fig.3.41　Composite fillet design (2)

In product design, as shown in Fig.3.42, small fillets in particular, are made with hyperbola according to the product structure and perspective relations.

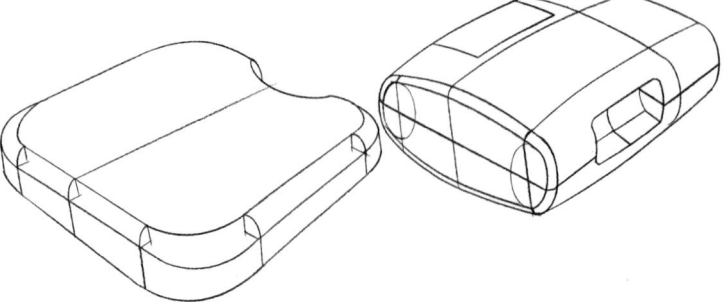
Fig.3.42　Composite fillet design in a product

Geometric surfaces

A geometric surface that is commonly applied to products, is a geometric plane that is regularly convex or regularly concave. This is how the surface modeling of a geometric shape is drawn, as shown in Fig.3.43 and Fig.3.44 — first draw a quadrilateral with perspective; second, set points and draw auxiliary lines; third, practise drawing the surface according to the horizontal plane or cross section.

The variations of the surface, although more complex and variable than basic geometric shapes, have their own rules. The ways to construct surfaces are as follow:

First, extruded surface. Stretch identical cross-sections in the same direction to form a curved surface, as shown in Fig.3.45.

Second, revolved surface. Revolve the cross-section around a central axis 360° to form a curved surface, as shown in Fig.3.46.

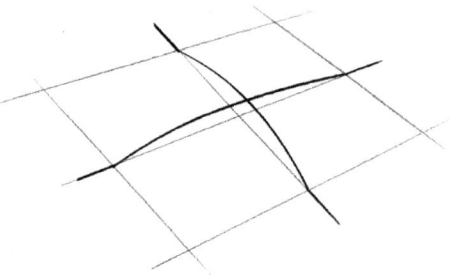

Fig.3.43 Convex surface

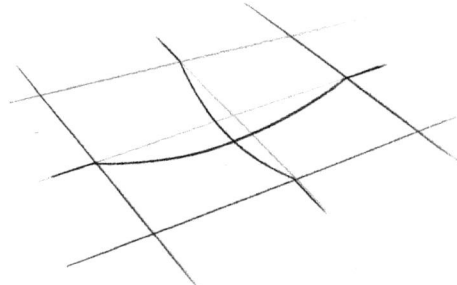

Fig.3.44 Concave surface

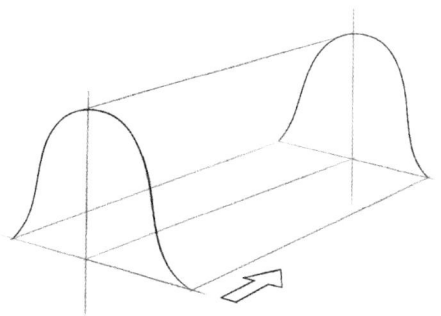

Fig.3.45 Extruded surface

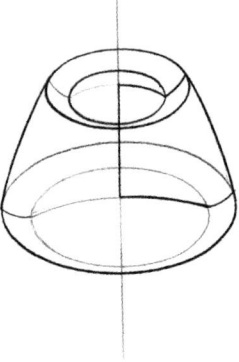

Fig.3.46 Revolved surface

Basics of Expression Techniques

Third, swept surface. As shown in Fig.3.47, a swept surface is formed by the movements of the cross-section along one or more directions.

Fourth, net surface. As shown in Fig.3.48, latitude and longitude lines interweave to form a net surface.

Fifth, surface combination. As shown in Fig.3.49 and Fig.3.50, a surface combination is formed by the intersection of multiple curved surfaces, and exhibits the characteristics of allotypic surfaces or streamlined surfaces.

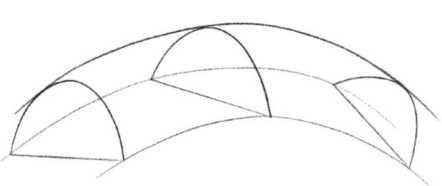

Fig.3.47   Swept surface

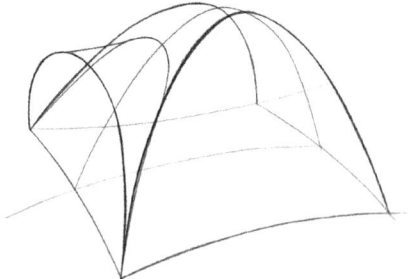

Fig.3.48   Net surface

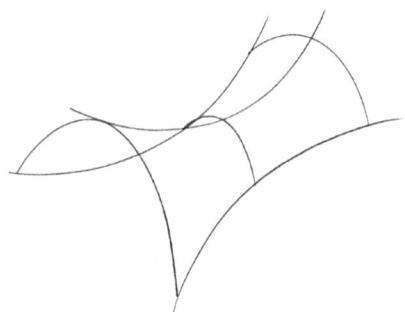

Fig.3.49   Surface combination (1)

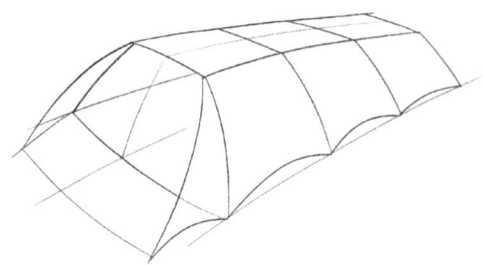

Fig.3.50   Surface combination (2)

Basics of Comprehensive Modeling Design

According to the definition of geometry, points move into a line, lines constitute a surface, and several surfaces make a cube, which three-dimensionally stems from the formation and motion of the surface. The structure is a starting point for understanding a solid. The key focus in basics of comprehensive modeling design is to analyze, simplify, and summarize the structure.

Surface rotation

As shown in Fig.3.51 to Fig.3.53, the rotation angle of the surface shown via perspective helps us analyze and express the product structure.

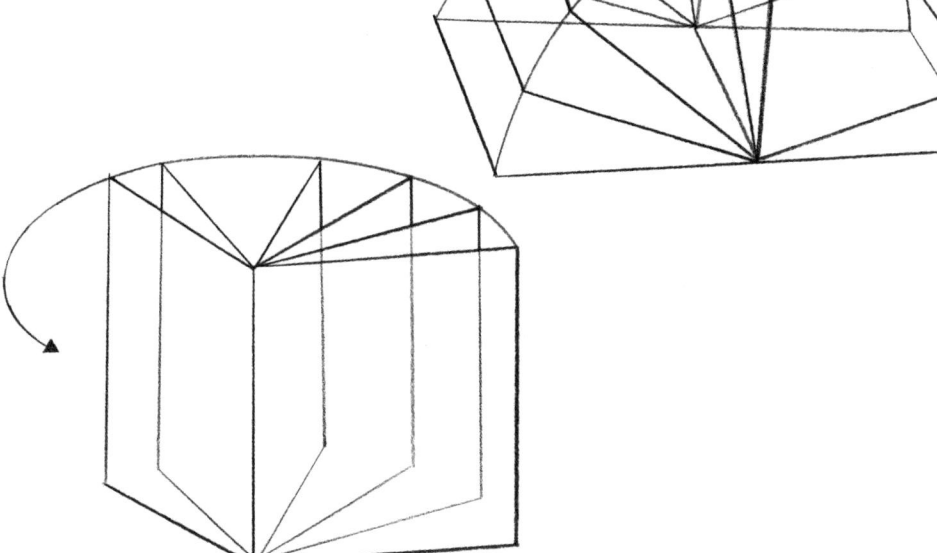

Fig.3.51 Surface rotation

Basics of Expression Techniques

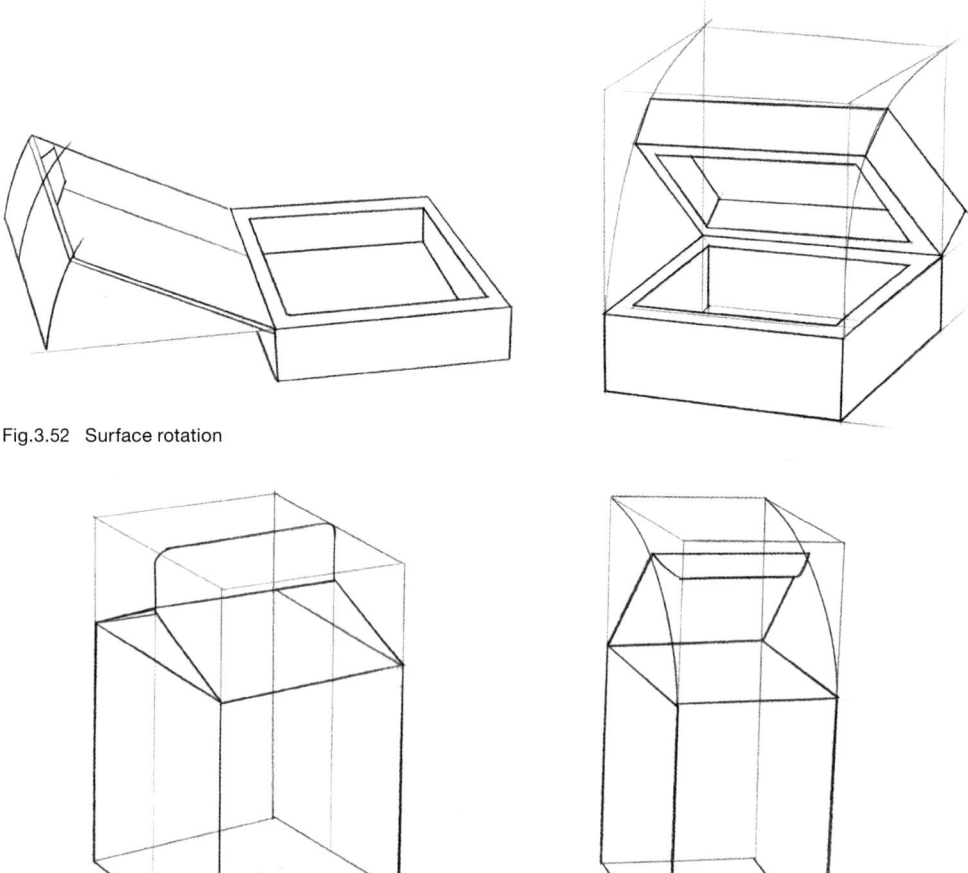

Fig.3.52 Surface rotation

Fig.3.53 Surface rotation

Structure analysis and simplification

Designers must analyze and simplify some complex structures for a better understanding of the product. For this reason, it is crucial to grasp this technique, the core of which is to figure out basic structural features behind a complicated appearance.

The structure of almost all complicated products need to be analyzed and simplified. To start with, we work out an analysis plan to find out the essentials and constitution of the structure. Secondly, we need to express it in a simplified way. A good understanding of the structural characteristics and details can help us to manipulate the complex structural form of the product, to better present the product modeling. For instance, as shown in Fig.3.54 to Fig.3.57, the complex structure of the kettle handle is firstly analyzed and then simplified by way of basic geometric structure.

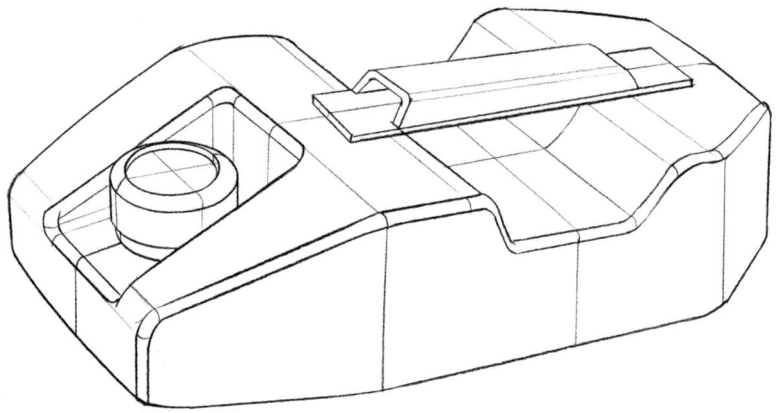

Fig.3.54 Kettle handle (1)

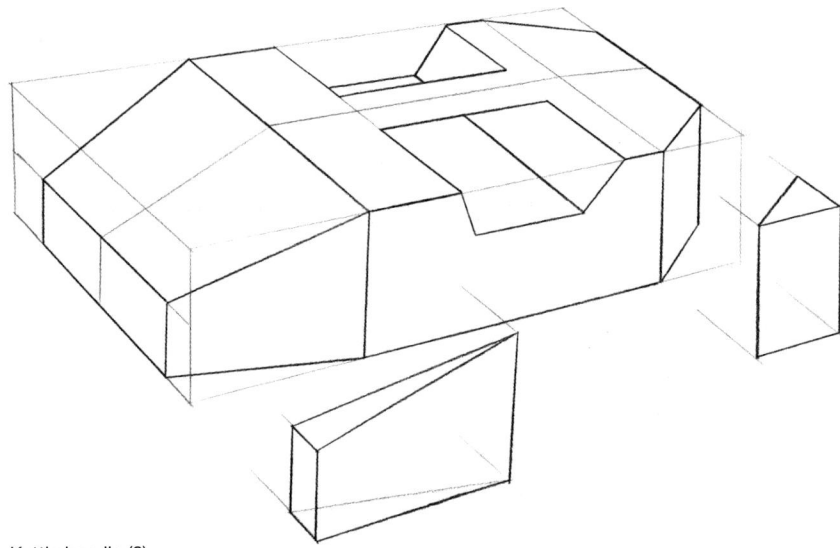

Fig.3.55 Kettle handle (2)

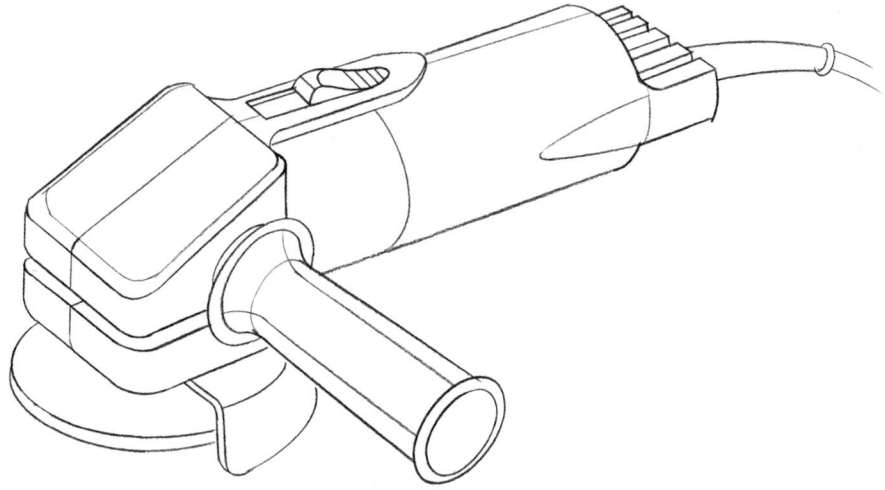

Fig.3.56   Kettle handle (3)

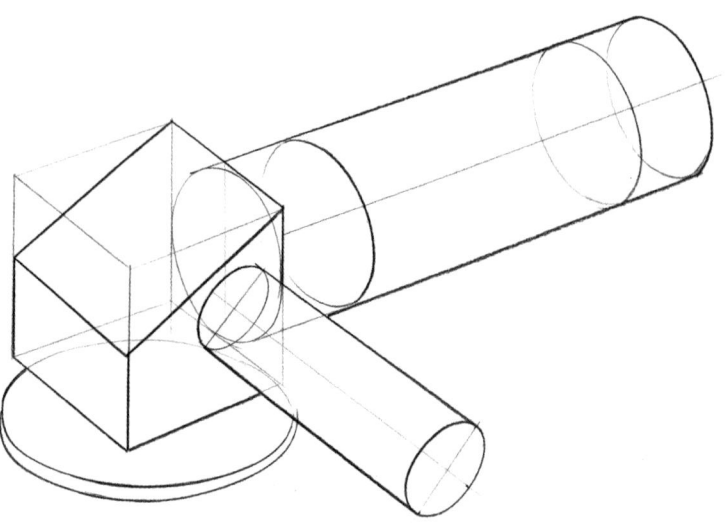

Fig.3.57   Kettle handle (4)

A Summary of Basic Skills

When practising basic skills, the following points should be noted:

1. Put effort into practise
Hand drawing expression techniques require half to one hour of practise every day, to draw more, memorize more, and think more. It is important to make this time in our daily routine. Like other design majors, hand drawing of products requires students to master basic skills soundly. The basic skill that kung fu practitioners should practise every day is their stance, painters should often practise sketching, similarly hand drawing requires daily practise for product designers to maintain these basic skills.

2. Crawl before you walk
Practise hand drawing expression techniques using products with a simple structure to start with. Observe before you draw, cultivate interest and confidence constantly. Beginners can practise by copying freehand from some copies, for example, some pictures featuring simple products. Later, draw directly from nature. Last, try to come up with a theme idea and create your own work.

3. Have patience and confidence
Doing an in-depth study is the premise to gain good proficiency over hand drawing expression techniques, during which a good balance and coordination should exist among brain, eyes and hands. The ability to balance and coordinate is only gained by prolonged practise. Those who overcome difficulties during learning with patience and confidence can perform hand drawing with great ease.

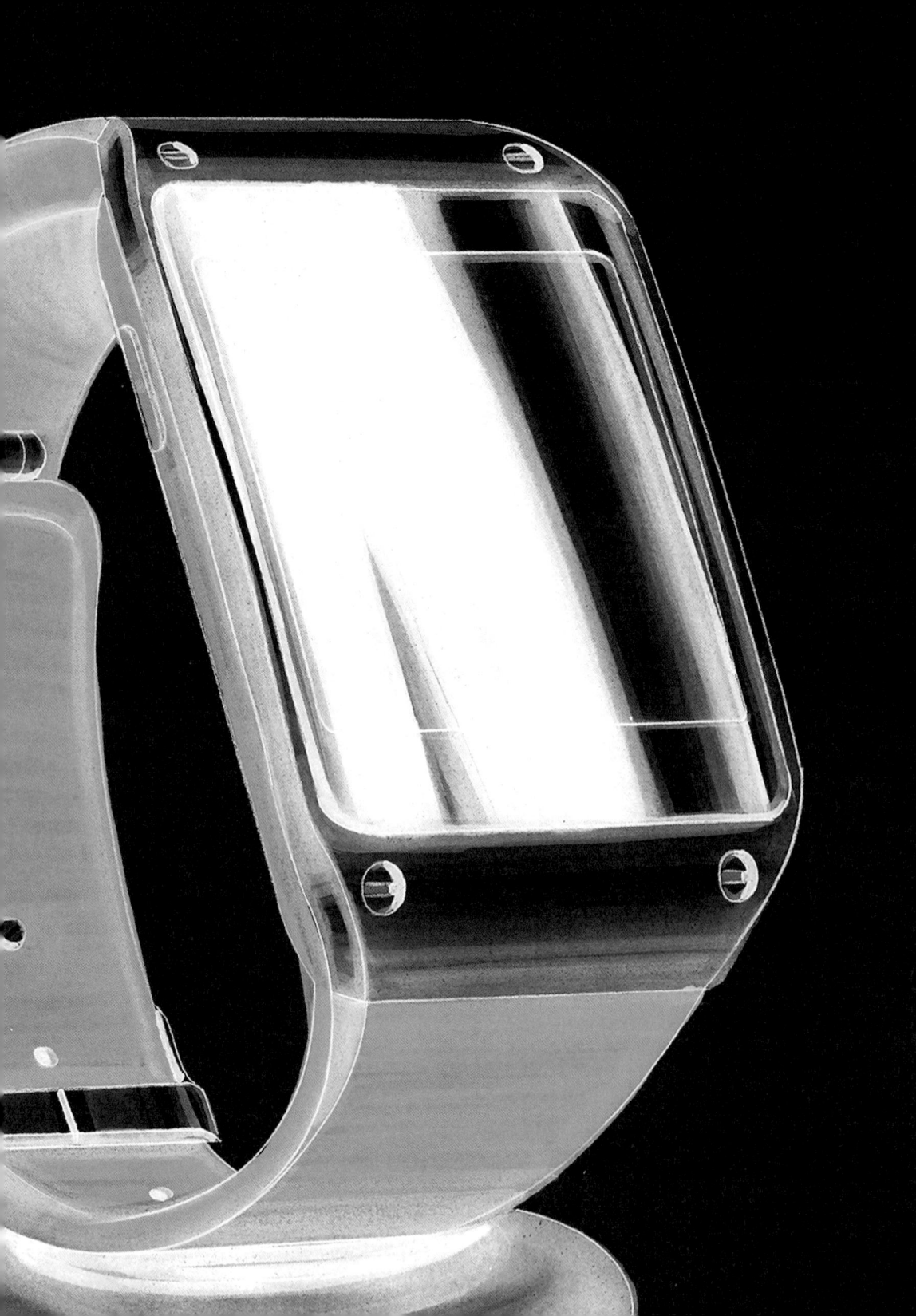

Expression Techniques of Product Material

CHAPTER 4

The material texture, texture for short, refers to the texture features of product and visual features of a processed surface. There are wide varieties of textures reflect multifarious texture features, like tough and soft, rough and smooth, transparent and opaque, and tight and fluffy. Furthermore, different processing methods and various texture treatments for the same material will produce different material effects. Texture expression is not only an important factor in product modeling design, but also a basic requirement of material performance in product rendering.

Material expression is categorized into three groups—reflective and opaque, reflective and light-transmittable, and the unreflective and opaque. Many tools can be used to express product material, including colored pencils, marker pens, toners, gouache, and etc.

This section focuses on marker pen expression techniques and introduces a form that combines multiple materials. Its typical features are its speed, convenience, and effect. Before learning material expression techniques, students must grasp some primary tips on usage of marker pens.

Application and Material Performance of Marker Pen

It's popularly known that you can't do a good freehand rendering of a product without marker pens. Marker pens have become essential in freehand rendering in all design specialties. Unlike paints, marker pens can easily provide the desired colors without color mixing. They are available in fixed color numbers, and can be used for color overlap to achieve the desired effects. Marker pens are capable of conveying the impression of colorful materials and lighting effects. They are preferred due to their good transmittance, excellent light resistance, high integration, and color stability. It is suggested that, beginners invest in a good set. These days, a huge range is available online as well, as shown in Fig.4.1 and Fig.4.2, designed for industrial designs or personal use.

Fig.4.1 Marker pens of various colors

Fig.4.2 Marker pens of various numbers

Practise the grip and strokes of marker pens

Before drawing freehand with a marker pen, maintain a correct sitting posture and hold the pen comfortably with arms resting on the desk. As shown in Fig.4.3, as the nib is beveled, the nib should be close to the paper at an angle of about 45° when drawing. Hold the paper down so it does not move. The pen strokes must be quick, or else the ink will permeate through paper and strokes will be distorted and smudge the writing paper. The kind of stroke required depends on the light source, form and material of the product. It is decided case-by-case, that is to say, there are no absolute rules. Before making the final stroke, it's advisable to practise strokes of various thickness, horizontal strokes, vertical strokes, curved strokes, gradient strokes, etc., repeatedly.

Strokes of various thickness: As shown in Fig.4.4, turn the tip of the marker pen to produce strokes of different thickness.

Horizontal stroke: Draw a rectangle outline with a pencil and then fill it with horizontal

Fig.4.3 Pen and paper at 45°

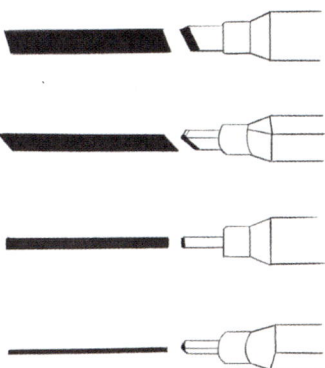

Fig.4.4 Strokes of various thickness

Expression Techniques of Product Material   065

Fig.4.5 Horizontal stroke

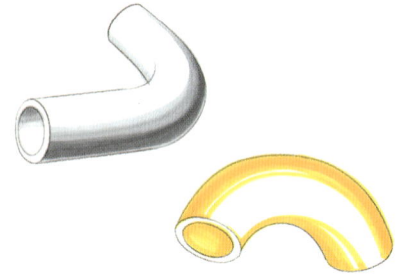

Fig.4.7 Curved stroke

Fig.4.8 Gradient stroke

strokes using a marker pen. Tips: first, wield the pen lightly; second, pay attention to the pressure applied on the pen at the beginning and end of its movement; third, make straight line strokes of uniform thickness; fourth, do not pause the pen on the paper; fifth, ensure all strokes are within the outline. As shown in Fig.4.5, coloring flat on the paper with Z shaped strokes blurs the superimposed marks between the lines.

Vertical stroke: Similar to the horizontal stroke, draw a pencil outline of a rectangle and fill it with vertical strokes using a marker pen. The strokes can be done in flat "M" strokes, as shown in Fig.4.6.

Curved stroke: Curved stroke is used mainly depending on the structure of modeling. As shown in Fig.4.7, the strokes of the marker pen must be made according to the shape of the surface of the product with no obvious pauses or strokes broken in the middle, to keep the shading of the surface of the product as smooth as possible.

Gradient stroke: Gradient stroke is a kind of stroke that gives light and shade gradient effect and is produced by marker pens. Types includes gray gradient and color gradient. The first step to produce gradient strokes is to select 3—5 marker pens of different shade from the same color scheme. First, color one-third of the square with a marker pen of the palest color. Before the ink dries up, color the next one-third of the square with a marker pen of the next darker shade, and so on. In this way you can create a gradient effect. Pay attention to the thickness of lines. At the boundaries of two different shade colors, overlap repeatedly over the paler color to create a gradient effect. The Fig.4.8 shows the watercolor-like gradient effect that can be acquired after a lot of practise.

Stroke direction: The stroke direction of the marker pen varies according to product modeling. As shown in Fig.4.9, there is a huge distinction over stroke directions among the three different models. For objects with obvious angular surfaces, like cubes, use perpendicular lines more since we need to differentiate each side for a better three-dimensional view of the sides. For cubes with composite fillets, primarily use oblique strokes and consider including light-and-shadow effects for a more obvious gradient effect. When filling ellipsoids, it is better to use curved strokes to highlight the entire structure. It is important to remember that stroke direction depends entirely on the person's preference, hence it is variable.

Fig.4.9 Stroke directions

Light and shade technique practise with marker pens

The light and shade effect arises from any opaque object under light and is summarized as three main sides to help us understand. Three main sides—the light side, the gray side, and the shadow side indicate the changes in the brightness of an object under the light. Usually, when drawing an object, you must consider the reflection of light, which is the light reflected on the object. To make a stereoscopic drawing, these three main sides could also be subdivided into five parts, which is the light side, the gray side, the shadow line, the shadow side and the reflected light. The light and shade technique is an effective way to present a 3-D effect.

Generally, there are two approaches to practise light and shade technique with marker pens—monochrome practise and hue practise.

Monochrome practise with marker pen: Roughly separate the light and the shade of product with gray marker pens before coloring. Note that it's not advisable to overlap color too much. It is better to neatly and swiftly overlay colors. Ensure that the paper is completely dry, or else the ink will smudge and destroy the neatness of the sketch. The advantages of marker pens here are the limpidity and neatness they impart to the sketch. For the most part, strokes are done in rows and are regular in their direction and their thickness so they appear uniform,

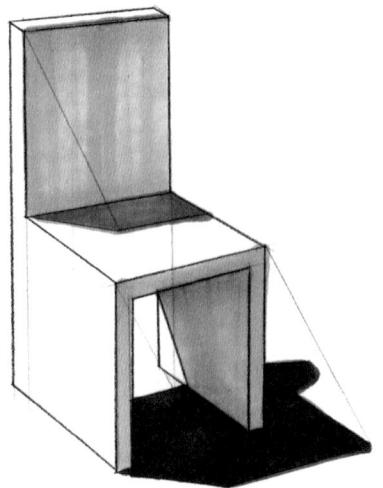
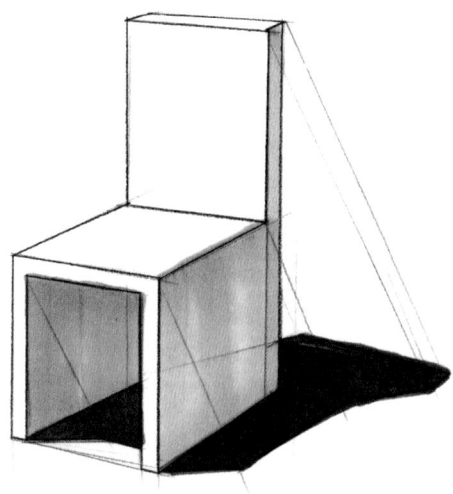

Fig.4.10 Monocrome shading with marker pens

Fig.4.11   Hue shading with marker pens (1)

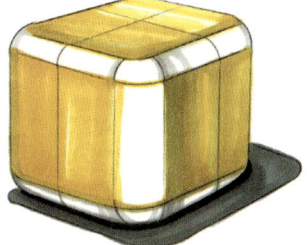

Fig.4.12   Hue shading with marker pens (2)

as shown in Fig.4.10. Pay attention to the coordination of colors and to the order of coloring, as a light color if used later cannot cover a dark color.

Hue practise with marker pen: Initially, practise with marker pens of different hues on the paper where you have sketched a model outline. This makes it easy and saves time as compared to making a copy via a copier or a light table. As shown in Fig.4.11 and Fig.4.12, hue practise with marker pens aims to imitate the identical hue of the model; hence it is more effective if we use marker pens of different hues.

Creating spatial volumes with marker pens

Drawing a model with marker pens can create spatial volumes , giving a sense of three-dimensionality. This technique improves our skills to express perspective relations and sense of space. We can show the relation of light and shade among spatial volumes and the differences of three main sides by using markers of light and dark colors, as shown in Fig.4.13 to Fig.4.18. It is advisable for beginners to start with practising simple geometric solids and gradually increase the difficulty.

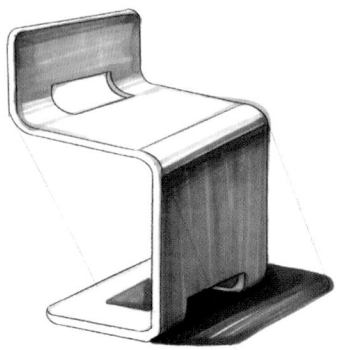

Fig.4.13 3D visualization using shading with marker pens (1)

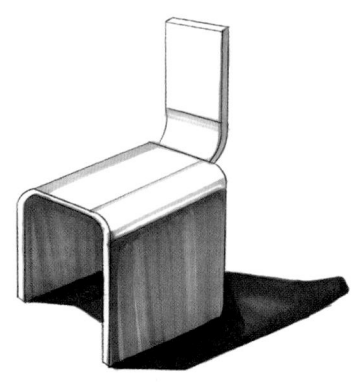

Fig.4.14 3D visualization using shading with marker pens (2)

Fig.4.15 3D visualization using shading with marker pens (3)

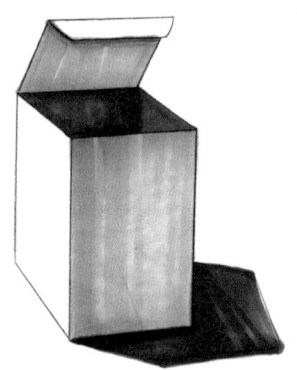

Fig.4.16 3D visualization using shading with marker pens (4)

070 SKETCH LIKE A PRO

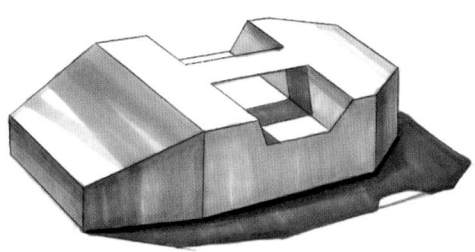

Fig.4.17 3D visualization using shading with marker pens (5)

Fig.4.18 3D visualization using shading with marker pens (6)

A summary of tips on usage of marker pens

Coloring with markers should be steady and fast without any hesitation. The direction of stroke depends on the direction of modeling, the shadow line, edges, and so on. Fillets or cambered surface need filling with to-and-fro strokes. Small corners or details need to be filled using the fine part of the pen point. While filling bigger areas, color along edges within first and then color the main body. For filling small objects such as buttons, just sketch around them with fine strokes. Overall, during coloring, we use only one hue, which is the main tone, matching it with two or three colors. Use marker pens from the same or similar scheme to cover the identical patch or the patch will look cloudy. Further, highlighting the relation of light and shade using markers helps to convey a three-dimensional sense, meanwhile using white space properly in the highlight part and the bends can make pictures look stereoscopic and natural.

Also, strokes need to vary appropriately in thickness, direction, density, length, etc. Last but not the least, illustrating with a highlight pen and colored pencil, highlight the details in the picture. The coloring effect of marker pens is different from that of other painting tools. Marker pens are ideal where the emphasis is on solid blocks, showcasing the relationship between light and shade and where we need not consider subtle color changes much.

Expression of Reflective and Opaque Material

Reflective but opaque materials are materials with smooth and opaque surfaces. Some common examples are stainless steel, copper, iron and other metal materials, smooth surface plastics, ceramics, and glass materials.

Fig.4.19 Hollow round stainless steel tubes

Fig.4.20 Metal round tubes

Expression techniques to depict metal material

Metal materials are widely used in product design for their hardness, fine texture, and surface smoothness. As shown in Fig.4.19 and Fig.4.20, metals, such as highly reflective stainless steel and chrome-plated metal have polished surfaces that reflect light.
This makes it challenging to decipher and depict the relations of light and shade in different surroundings.

How do we express metal materials with marker pens? Firstly, note the position of the light source, identify the highlight part, the shadow edge area, the reflected light part, and the cast shadow. Next, analyze, simplify, and generalize the light source on the metal surface, omit superfluous light, and strengthen the contrast between light and shadow. Additionally, as shown in Fig.4.21 and Fig.4.22, due to their characteristic features, most metal materials have strong highlights, you must emphasize the dark part, use white space extensively and use strokes

  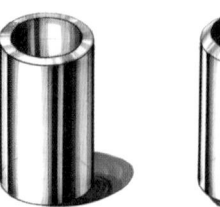 

Fig.4.21 Depicting metallic surface with marker pens

072   SKETCH LIKE A PRO

that are neat and flat with clear edges. For beginners, it's a good idea to find pictures of products made of metal on the internet or in real life, such as hot water bottles, faucets, thermos bottles, and practise using them. Make sure that the pictures you choose as beginners must have the following elements.

1. Appropriate perspective: the best perspective shows exterior features of the product to the maximum without ambiguity.

2. Uniform light sources: for beginners, a single light source will be better, because too many light sources complicate the effect, which might lead to a distorted drawing when attempted by a beginner.

3. Relatively simple product structure and a single product material: as shown in Fig.4.23 to Fig.4.26, it's advisable that beginners choose products with a relatively simple structure to practise with, preferably made of a single material, and then gradually move to products made of multiple materials.

Fig.4.23 Stainless steel electric kettle

Fig.4.24 Hand-drawn sketch of the stainless steel electric kettle using marker pens

Fig.4.25 Stainless steel faucet

Fig.4.26 Hand-drawn sketch of the faucet with marker pens

Expression Techniques of Product Material 073

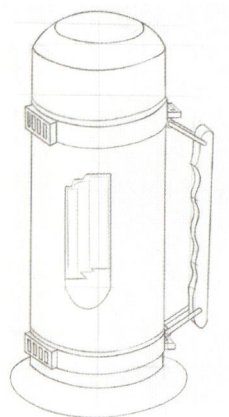
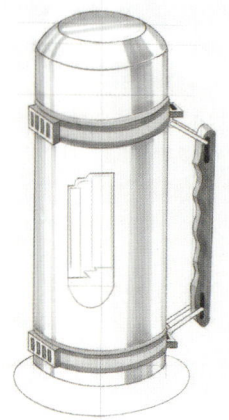

Fig.4.27 Thermos vacuum flask

Fig.4.28 Sketch of the thermos vacuum flask

Fig.4.29 Filling in the details with marker pens

You need to focus on the following aspects while drawing using pictures.

1. Observe, think as well as use your hands, that is you must draw after a careful observation and analysis of the features and structure of the model product. (Analyze the structure first.)

2. Analyze the positions of light sources and some key elements including the light side, the space in-between the bright and the dark, the transitional part and the reflected light area.

3. Strive to create neat and fluid strokes, and add details in place using marker pens.

The next phase after practising drawing using pictures is sketching by looking at material objects, as shown in Fig.4.27. The specific steps are as follows.

Step 1: Draw a sketch. To begin with, observe the structural features of a thermos vacuum flask and analyze what kind of geometric solid that flask is like. Next, analyze the relations of perspective and structure from a proper observing position. Lastly, complete an outline drawing. In this case, the object is a vacuum flask, whose body is a cylinder; the top is a cone as seen from the cross-section. The difficulty lies in the curved section of the handle, where the perspective relationship is needed while drawing this challenging part. Furthermore, as shown in Fig.4.28, you also should note the product composition, proportion and other external features.

Step 2: Color the background with marker pens. First, analyze material features including light sources and the relations of light and shade, and then roughly distinguish the light side from the shadow side using gray series marker pens. During this step, just fill and you do not need to emphasis

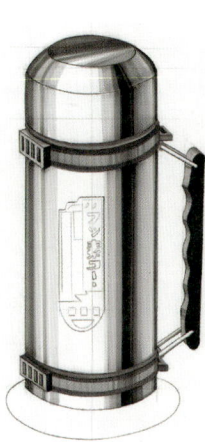

Fig.4.30 Chiaroscuro created with marker pens

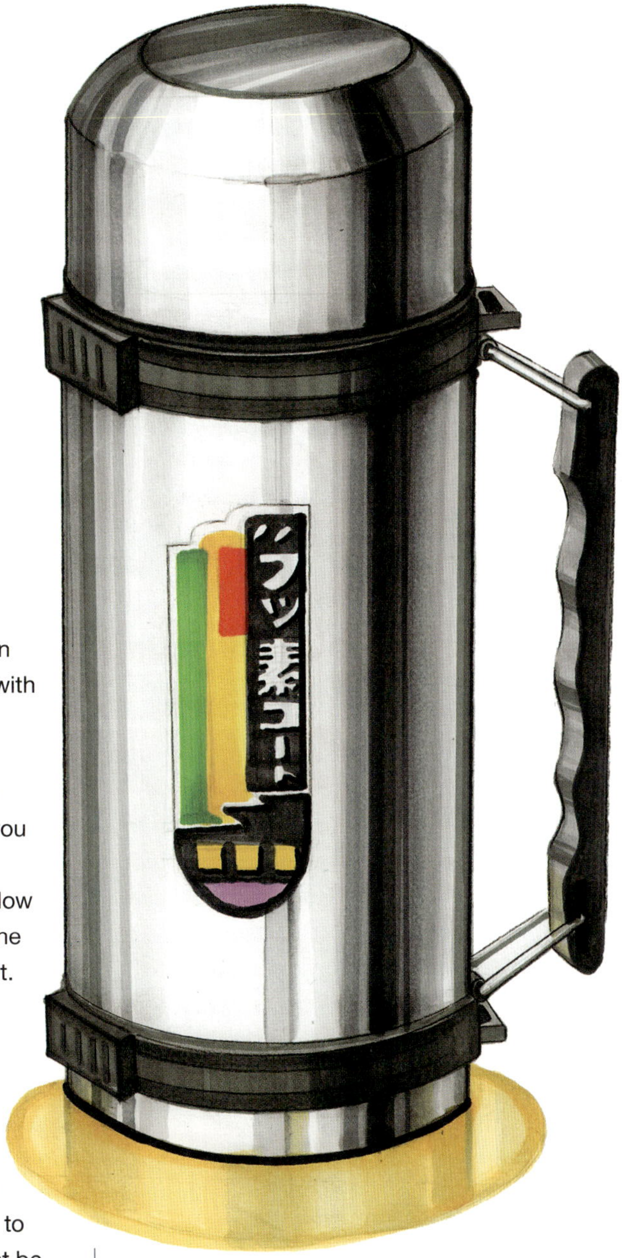

on details. You need to follow some rules while coloring. Lastly, as shown in Fig.4.29, progressively overlay colors with marker pens of dark color.

Step 3: Intensify Chiaroscuro. Make a further analysis of material features—you must leave white space on the lit light side, blacken the dark part of the shadow line area, and add gradient effects in the transitional part and reflected light part. Highlight the metal surface with high contrast, as shown in Fig.4.30.

Step 4: Refine details. Draw details and the cast shadow on the ground. A trick to do it faster is to successfully complete details starting from outside to inside. However, the cast shadow must be drawn carefully. As you can see in Fig.4.31, it is better to use a pastel color in the cast shadow that matches the main color to prevent too much contrast.

Fig.4.31 Adding finer details

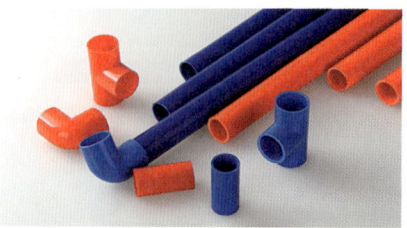

Fig.4.32 Smooth plastic

Fig.4.33 Frosted plastic

Expression techniques to depict plastic surface

According to the processing method, plastic surfaces can be smooth or frosted. We need different kinds of marker pens to create the effect of these two kinds of plastic. Smooth plastic is the plastic whose surface is quite smooth and highly reflective after special processing. It is because of its properties that smooth plastic is widely used in products. Frosted plastic is a plastic whose surface is rather rough and barely reflective, therefore it is similar to rubber and argil (pottery clay). As you can see in Fig.4.32 and Fig.4.33, highlights barely exist on the surface of frosted plastic, so there is not much contrast between light and shade on plastic.

There are many similarities in depicting the surface of smooth plastic and metal material. However, the intrinsic colors of smooth plastic need to be much more saturated. Smooth plastic looks mild and the light and shade contrast of it is not as great as that of metal material. You can leave white spaces moderately within the highlight part and the reflected light part, like in the metal material. As shown in Fig.4.34, when drawing a smooth surface with marker pens, attention should be given to black, white, and gray contrasts, highlights and reflected light.

Compared with the texture of smooth material, there is no white space within the highlight part and less reflection on the surface of frosted plastic. More grays are

Fig.4.34 Depicting smooth plastic surface with marker pens

Fig.4.35 Depicting frosted plastic surface with marker pens

integrated in the intrinsic color for lesser brightness and purity of tone. Do not use more than three colors, or the sketch may not appear pleasing. As shown in Fig.4.35, the strokes of markers in frosted plastic drawing are softer and applied many more times. To practise drawing plastic materials, you can use some pictures of plastic products as a model. This practising lays the foundation for later product sketching because it helps in understanding and analyzing product structure as well as to grasp the basic rules of material expression. When you practise using a picture, don't use the same color as in the picture. Instead, draw on the basis of understanding, analysis, rules of material expression, even without referring back to the picture, till you complete the sketch. Draw without referring but use your own understanding to express the product's material features, and then analyze by comparing your drawing with the original picture. As shown in Fig.4.36 to Fig.4.41, you can select a similar color as in the picture, or a nearest color from another scheme to represent the color in the picture if a similarly colored marker pen is not available. You can also practise this part using the hue practise mentioned in the previous chapter.

Fig.4.36 Vacuum cleaner

Fig.4.37 Sketch of the vacuum cleaner drawn with marker pens

Expression Techniques of Product Material

Fig.4.38 Rice cooker

Fig.4.39 Sketch of the rice cooker drawn with marker pens

Fig.4.40 Laundry detergent bottle

Fig.4.41 Sketch of the laundry detergent bottle drawn with marker pens

Next, after practising drawing a picture, practise sketches of specific products, as shown in Fig.4.42. The steps are as follows.

Step 1: Draw a sketch. For this table lamp, firstly you need to analyze its modeling features and geometric compositions. Secondly, start your outline drawing, observing from a good perspective. To get a successful outline drawing of the lamp, you need to understand the elliptic perspective of the lampshade and the annular supporting column. Then draw the outline image in a simplified and summarized way. The power cord at the bottom right of the lamp can be ignored when you detail the image, as shown in Fig.4.43.

Step 2: Color the background with marker pens. In this case, the lampshade and lamp holder are both made of smooth plastic, whereas the surface of the column is made of soft rubber, which could be viewed as frosted plastic. These two materials are expressed differently. Firstly, start coloring the background with red and gray series marker pens, except the highlight part. During coloring, make sure to use thicker strokes closer to the transitional area between the light side and the shadow side,

Fig.4.42 Table lamp

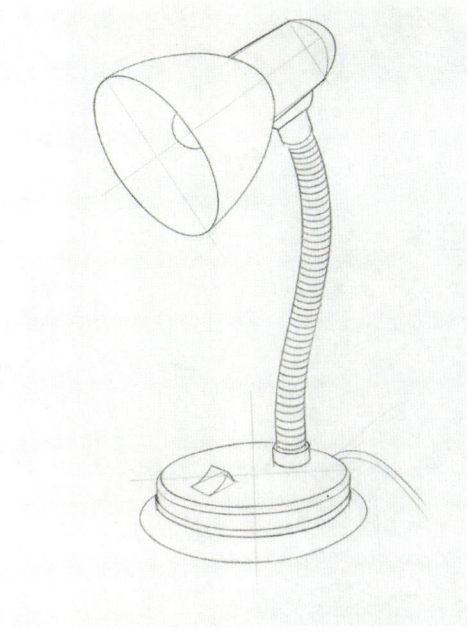

Fig.4.43 A freehand outline sketch of the table lamp

Expression Techniques of Product Material **079**

thinner strokes closer to the highlight part. Secondly, as shown in Fig.4.44, focus on the whole image, not so much the finer details.

Step 3: Enhance chiaroscuro to highlight the material features, and then make further detailing of material features. Create a full gradient effect from the highlight part to the area where the bright-dark shadings meet in the transitional area. Leave some white space in the highlight part of smooth plastic to give the impression of depth. Since the material of the lamp column is frosted plastic, you do not have to leave white space in the highlight part. Ensure that the light-shade contrast is formed such that the cylinder looks solid. The color and modeling are mutually coordinated in this sketch. When expressing two different materials with markers, as shown in Fig.4.45, try to ensure they match and not use too much contrast, to avoid the picture from looking inconsistent and lacking in aesthetics.

Step 4: Manage the additional details. As shown in Fig.4.46, the inside surface of the lampshade and the cast shadow part are painted in yellow marker pens, and details like the switch and wire are added. This makes the image more realistic. Usually,

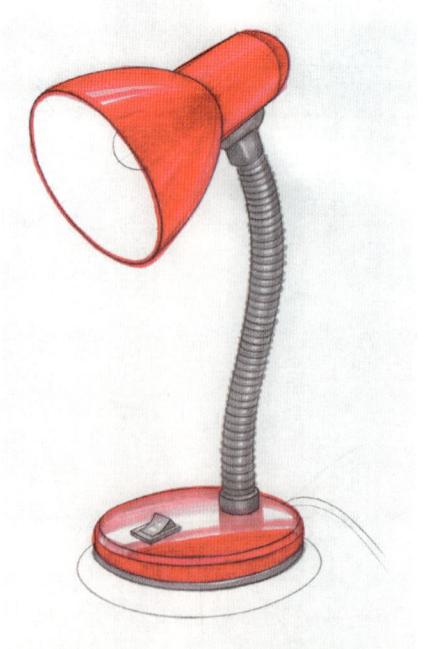

Fig.4.44 Coloring details achieved using marker pens

Fig.4.45 Chiaroscuro using marker pens

Fig.4.46 Adding finer details

when creating the impression of plastic, highlight the intrinsic colors of the material and use shades within the range of the intrinsic colors. In other words, when the lampshade and lamp holder are both red plastic, these two parts must be painted in red series with no other colors from other series, even if the colors look somewhat different in their surroundings. Practise using a variety of marker pens from the red series to convey the effect of gradients. It is important to master the technique of creating a gradient effect in colors from the same series.

Expression Techniques of Product Material 081

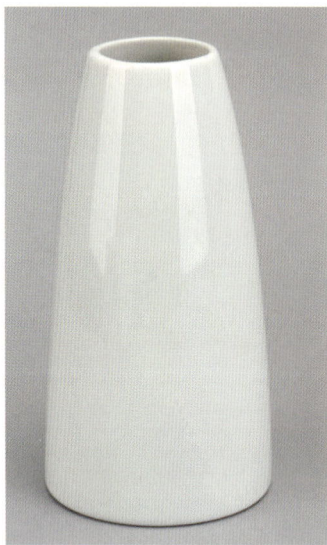

Fig.4.47   Porcelain material

Fig.4.48   Pottery material

Expression technique to depict ceramic material

Ceramic material is divided into pottery and porcelain based on the material composition and production process. Pottery has a rough, grainy and usually brown surface, giving a vintage feel and uneven appearance, while the bright and smooth surface and fine texture of porcelain gives a feeling of gentleness and softness. Although there are some obvious differences between pottery and porcelain, they still have some similarities—neutral colors of the overall tone. They have neither strong chiaroscuro like metal material nor gorgeous coloring like plastic material, as shown in Fig.4.47 and Fig.4.48. Simplistic approaches are ideal to express ceramic material with marker pens. There is much white space in the highlight part; and try to use a light-colored marker in the transitional area between the highlight and shadow line. The boundary area of light and shade should not be too obvious, and a small amount of reflective effect is better. In this way, the ceramic material looks brighter and more transparent.

Here are some pictures for practise, as shown in Fig.4.49 to Fig.4.52. The phase after practising drawing using pictures is practising sketches of a specific product. Here is a common white porcelain teapot, as shown in Fig.4.53.

The teapot looks wide and flat. The slightly rising spout, on the left side, is flush with the mouth. The mildly upward handle, on the right side, is squarish and round. The left and right side of the teapot are symmetrical

082   SKETCH LIKE A PRO

and the shape is very stable. Therefore, the sketch should be concise, fluent, and symmetrical. The color of this teapot is white, the surface appears clean, bright, and smooth. So, when drawing with marker pens, you should choose gray as the main color. From the material, first you can see that the light source is reflected on the teapot. It looks like the top half of the teapot is in the lit side. You need to set your own tones including highlight area, shadow line area, transitional area, reflected light area, and cast shadow, and remove the confounding light source.

Then, observe the texture. It is important to depict the reflective surface in the gray tone of the teapot, in other words, the relationship of highlight area and reflected light area should be accurately handled. The specific steps to achieve this are as follows.

Fig.4.51 Clay pot

Fig.4.49 Porcelain cup

Fig.4.50 Freehand sketch of the porcelain cup done with marker pens

Fig.4.52 Freehand sketch of the clay pot done with marker pens

Expression Techniques of Product Material 083

Fig.4.53 White porcelain teapot

Fig.4.54 Outline sketch of the porcelain teapot

Step 1: Draw a sketch. First analyze the features of the teapot and select a proper perspective to draw a sketch. When drawing the teapot, you need to understand and depict the perspective of the ellipse, as shown in Fig.4.54.

Step 2: Color the background with marker pens. The ceramic material gives the teapot a smooth and delicate surface, which creates a feeling of mildness and tenderness. So, the overall tone of the teapot should be in neutral colors, with neither great chiaroscuro nor flamboyant tint. For this reason, it would be a good choice to select off-white as the preferred tone. You can use gray markers to color a large area. Don't forget to leave white space in highlight areas. Don't make the bright-dark junction areas too obvious , and create the gradients carefully, as shown in Fig.4.55.

Step 3: Show the gradient effect of light and shade and refine details. To highlight the characteristics of porcelain ware, a little white space should be left in the highlight

Fig.4.55 Detailing added

part and create the gradient effect in the space in-between the bright and the dark. Take care to ensure it looks balanced. The shadow side should not be too dark, and the reflective effect should be maintained. The last step is to draw the cast shadow at the base of the teapot to make the picture more stereoscopic, as shown in Fig.4.56.

Pottery material is rougher than porcelain material and it's not a reflective surface. We are not giving an in-depth analysis in this section. You can refer to the earlier introduction about the techniques of expressing textures of materials.

Fig.4.56 Completed sketch with detailing made with marker pen

Expression technique of glass

Glass, also reflective and opaque materials, is mainly used in TV screens, LCDs, reflectors and other related products, as shown in Fig.4.57 to Fig.4.60.

The technique of depicting glass is similar to that of metal surfaces, as glass also has a fine, smooth and highly reflective surface. It is usually depicted by regular hatching with different colored marker pens. Mirror effect depends much on the light-shadow contrast. So, the flow of strokes should be smooth,

Fig.4.57 Old convex screen TV

Fig.4.58 LCD TV

Fig.4.59 Smartwatch

Expression Techniques of Product Material **085**

Fig.4.60 Convex road safety mirror

and the gradations of dark should be clear. Avoid messy lines as they can damage the effect. As shown in Fig.4.61, the same glass surface can be presented in different ways with changes of light and shadow. Let's do a light source analysis. In the picture, for the first mirror, the light source comes directly above it. Horizontal strokes are used to show gradual change. For the second mirror in the middle, the light source comes from the left. It's effective to use oblique strokes to show gradient. The light source of the third mirror comes from both the left and right sides. The vertical stroke is a better choice. Keep in mind that the direction of stroke depends not only on the position of the light source but also on the surroundings and the shape of lights. Therefore, you need to analyze on a case-by-case basis.

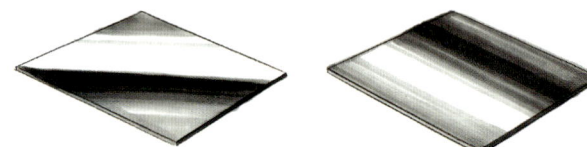

Fig.4.61 Creating a glass surface impression with marker pens

The glass material can be divided into horizontal plane and curved surface. Let us analyze curved mirror imaging through a reflector, as shown in Fig.4.62.

Fig.4.62 Reflector

As shown in Fig.4.63, the horizontal plane usually reflects what the surrounding scenery really looks like, while a curved surface generally compresses the reflected scenery inward or extends it outward to form a new anamorphic image. So, when drawing with marker pens, you have to not only represent the curved lines at the edges but show the compressed image.

Fig.4.63 Depicting a curved glass surface using marker pens

Spherical and convex mirror surfaces are common. Analyzing how the surroundings are reflected in these pictures can help us understand the effect of imaging, as shown in Fig.4.64 and Fig.4.65. In Fig.4.66, we can see that considerable differences exist among the images of a spherical surface, convex surface, conical mirror, and the imaging of a flat mirror surface. The imaging of a spherical mirror surface is in the shape of 360° rotation and stretch. The imaging of a convex mirror surface is in the form of arc stretching, wide at both ends and narrow in the middle, while the imaging of a conical mirror surface is radial, which radiates from the conical point outwards.

Fig.4.64 Sphere with a reflective surface

Fig.4.65 Convex mirror

Fig.4.66 Reflective surfaces of a hollow sphere, convex and conical curved surfaces using marker pens

Expression Techniques of Product Material **087**

Fig.4.67 Smartwatch

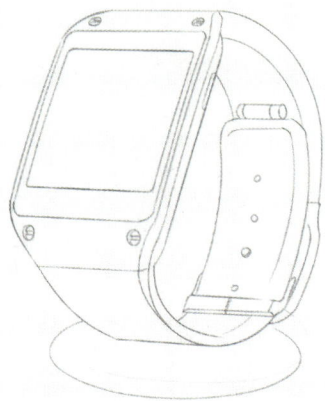

Fig.4.68 Outline sketch of the smartwatch

Now let's analyze the techniques to depict the glass surface of a smartwatch, as shown in Fig.4.67. The design of this smartwatch is not so complicated. The main shape of the watch is close to a cuboid and the bracelet similar to an annular cylinder. The watch consists of three materials: the glass display of the screen, the metal of the watch-face and the frosted plastic of the strap. We must clearly differentiate these three materials using marker pens. The glass surface should be flat, smooth, bright, and clean. Chiaroscuro and reflection should be shown in the metal part. Frosted plastic should be represented by intrinsic color and low reflection. The overall image must appear clear and fluent. Specific steps to do this are as follows:

Step 1: Draw an outline sketch of the smartwatch. First observe the features of the smartwatch and then draw it with clear and smooth lines, as shown in Fig.4.68. You can additionally use rulers.

Step 2: Use marker pens to create the glass surface of the smartwatch screen. The smartwatch screen has a fine, smooth, and reflective surface. Use different shades of gray markers for hatching. However, there are a few things you need to pay attention to. First, the strong contrast of light and shade should be emphasized in the flat mirror surface. Second, the flow of strokes should be smooth. Third, the chiaroscuro should be clear with distinct highlight and reflected light part, as shown in Fig.4.69.

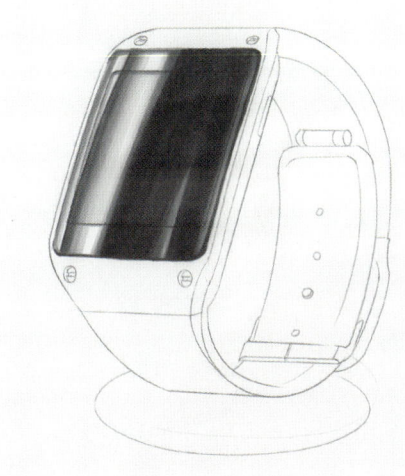

Fig.4.69 Detailing the smartwatch screen using marker pens

Fig.4.70 Metallic surface impression created with marker pens

Step 3: Use marker pens to depict the metal texture of the face of the smartwatch. It is useful to understand the characteristics of the metal surface to depict the texture. Leave white space in the highlight areas of the metal. Exaggerate the highlight part and the space in-between the bright and the dark. Create gradient effect in the transitional area and reflected light area. Use thick strokes, as shown in Fig.4.70.

Step 4: Use marker pens to depict the plastic surface of the smartwatch. The strap of the smartwatch is made of matte plastic, with low highlight and reflection. We can create the structure and texture of the strap by showing the intrinsic color and light and shade contrast. As shown in Fig.4.71.

Fig.4.71 Impression of plastic surface created with marker pens

Expression Techniques of Product Material

Step 5: Accentuate chiaroscuro and refine details. Lastly, further accentuate the relations between various materials. Take care not to overdo it, as too much contrast can lead to an incongruous and unaesthetic image. Use a few highlight lines with white colored pencils to refine details and draw cast shadow at the base of the smartwatch to make the picture more stereoscopic, as shown in Fig.4.72.

Fig.4.72 Final sketch with chiaroscuro and finer details

Expression of Reflective and Transparent Materials

Reflective and transparent materials refer to those materials with bright, reflective, and transparent surfaces. Common examples of such materials are glass, transparent plastic, as shown in Fig.4.73 and Fig.4.74.

Both glass and transparent plastics have high reflection and refraction, with strong highlights, clear edges, rich light and shadows and excellent transmittance. When drawing, you can depict the the shape and thickness of the products. Emphasize contours, light and shadow, and highlight and reflected light part according to the surroundings or internal structure of the product itself. Notice that you need to depict the perspective lines and components of the inner surface to show transparency.

Fig.4.73 Glass products

Fig.4.74 Transparent plastic products

Additionally, to highlight the feature of transparency, draw a simple background so that the highlight area of transparent materials stands out.

The cast shadow of a transparent object is often lighter in color than the object, as shown in Fig.4.75 to Fig.4.80.

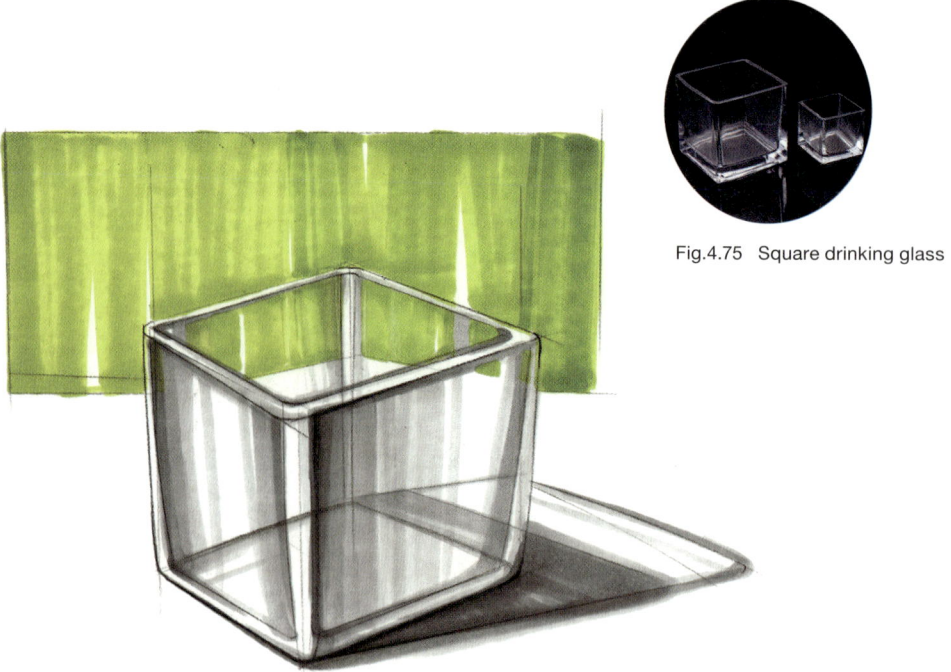

Fig.4.75 Square drinking glass

Fig.4.76 Sketch of square drinking glass created with marker pens

Fig.4.77 Round drinking glass

Fig.4.79 Beverage bottle

Fig.4.78 Sketch of round drinking glass created with marker pens

Fig.4.80 Sketch of the beverage bottle created wiith marker pens

Now let's analyze the expression techniques of reflective and transparent materials using this transparent water bottle as an example, as shown in Fig.4.81.

The basic shape of this transparent bottle is a cylinder with a large lower body and a small upper part. It is composed of five parts: spout, lid, body, corded tag, and handle, which are made of plastic, transparent plastic and soft cord. When drawing with marker pens, we must differentiate the texture of these three materials. Among them, plastic material has a rougher surface. So, it's necessary to show chiaroscuro and inherent color. Depicting transparent plastic material requires emphasis on the transparency and light-and-shadow effects, so the strokes should be minimal. In this example, the cord is a crucial feature, hence you just need to draw the lines clearly and to coordinate it with the rest of the image as much as possible.

Expression Techniques of Product Material 093

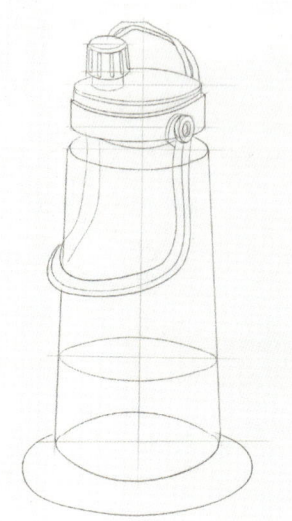
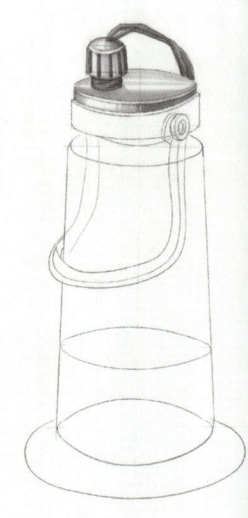

Fig.4.81 Transparent water bottle

Fig.4.82 Outline sketch of the transparent water bottle

Fig.4.83 Detailing on the spout and lid of the bottle done with marker p

The specific steps are as follows.

Step 1: Draw an outline sketch of the bottle. Analyze the features of the bottle, and then draw it with clear and smooth lines, as shown in Fig.4.82. You can additionally use rulers.

Step 2: Use marker pens to draw the spout and lid. The basic form of the spout is a cylinder, with a groove on the surface. Use dark gray marker pens to draw the groove and create a bright-dark gradient for the whole spout. Draw the upper part of the lid using horizontal strokes with marker pens. The strokes must be in a gradient of thickness and thinness. Leave the highlight part with some white space, as shown in Fig.4.83. The cord part can be done with a single light shade, to make it not too obvious.

Step 3: Use marker pens to draw the handle. The shape of the handle is an irregular curved surface. So, you need to pay attention to the width and the direction of the curved surface. Additionally, the handle is made of plastic and a part of it is blocked by the body. It should have contrasting brightness, as shown in Fig.4.84.

Step 4: Use marker pens to depict the transparent plastic material. The body is made of transparent plastic material. Note that you don't have to draw thick lines on the side. Secondly, as the body is very

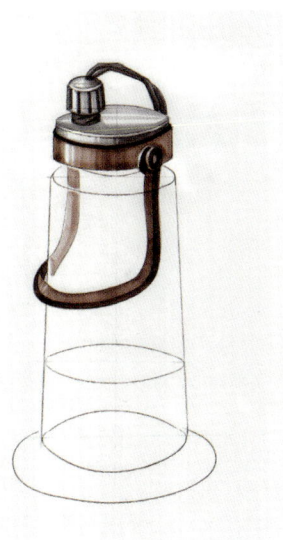

Fig.4.84 Details of the bottle handle done with marker pens

transparent, you have to contrast only between the left inner wall and the right outer wall and the stroke must be mild. Thirdly, you don't need to highlight the light and shadow of the water as this can be achieved by reflecting the surface of the water, as shown in Fig.4.85.

We can see from this example that transparent material is easier to depict. In summary, firstly, a lot of complicated highlights exist in transparent objects, we only need to depict them well. Secondly, the renders should be properly blurred and deformed when drawing as the internal structure and the object in the back can be seen through transparent material. Thirdly,

Fig.4.85 Completed details of transparent bottle using marker pens

it is better to use gradients for the drawing since it is similar to light and shadow effect; this is due to uneven cast shadow of the transparent material.

Expression of Non-reflective and Opaque Material

The non-reflective and lightproof material means that the surface of the material does not reflect light and is opaque due to its material properties. This kind of material can be subdivided into soft non-reflective and opaque material and hard non-reflective and opaque material.

Technique of depicting soft non-reflective and opaque material

The soft non-reflective and opaque material is mainly characterized by even absorbency, no reflection, no light transmission, and soft surface. Textures like cloth, leather, rubber, sponge, etc. are some examples, as shown in Fig.4.86.

It's challenging to depict this kind of material with marker pens, for you not only have to show the fine and delicate quality but also the softness. In this section, fabric and leather are mainly analyzed in detail. When depicting cloth surface with marker pens, try to color evenly, apply the pen strokes longer to make the picture fully wet, and keep the lines soft and smooth to avoid too many edges and corners. The chiaroscuro should not be too strong with appropriate highlights.

Fig.4.86 Cloth

Fig.4.87 Leather

Fig.4.88 Rubber

Fig.4.89 Sponge

Fig.4.90 Fabric sofa

Fig.4.91 Impression of fabric surface created with marker pens

Add some decorative details if necessary, as shown in Fig.4.90 and Fig.4.91.

Now let's analyze the expression techniques of cloth material using the example of a single fabric sofa, as shown in Fig.4.92.

The shape of this single sofa is like a square. The raised backrest, cushion and armrest are soft. The cambered armrests on the two sides are wrinkled; making it harder to depict.

The single sofa is basically made of cloth, with light gray fabric. So, when representing cloth with marker pens, you need to show the softness on the whole product, and color evenly. Chiaroscuro is allowed but should not be too strong. Marker pens can be used to draw curved strokes to represent the bulging backrest and elastic cushion. Use cross-hatching to show decorative details on the fabric. The specific steps are as follows.

Fig.4.92 Single fabric sofa

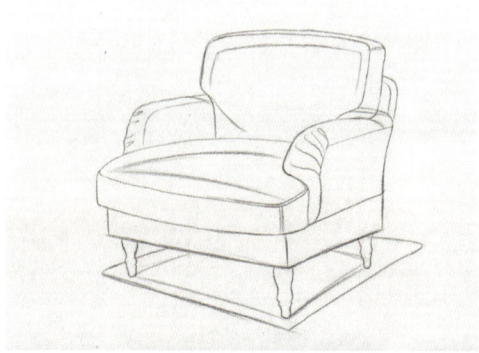

Fig.4.93 Outline a sketch of the single fabric sofa

Fig.4.94 Color effect done with marker pens

Fig.4.95 Chiarocuro detailing added

Step 1: Draw an outline sketch of the sofa. Analyze the features of the single sofa and then draw it with clear and smooth lines, as shown in Fig.4.93.

Step 2: Use gray marker pens to show the dominant color of the sofa. The key point of this step is to draw strokes smoothly and fast without any hesitation or pauses. Firstly, distinguish the contrast effect of each side of the sofa and keep details to the minimum. Secondly, control the direction of your strokes with the marker pens. To depict the bulging backrest and cushion, you draw curved lines and gradients, leaving some white space as needed, as shown in Fig.4.94.

Step 3: Detail the light and shade relations. In this step, you need to detail the light and shade relations between various parts. Try not to overdo this, as too much contrast makes the image incongruous and unaesthetic. Besides, when drawing with marker pens, use strokes with gradual changes of density and thickness to represent the softness and texture of cloth.

Moreover, lighter marker pens can be used to draw cross-hatching to represent the decorations, as shown in Fig.4.95.

Step 4: Refine details. Firstly, use cross-hatching to depict the fabric texture.

Additionally, black and white pencils can be used to draw stitches and highlights. Lastly, paint the cast shadow of the sofa. In this way, the marker depiction of the single sofa is completed, as shown in Fig.4.96.

Fig.4.96 Finer details added

When using marker pens to present leather material, you must not only express the softness and the sense of fullness, but also to show the smoothness of the texture and reflection. Therefore, while coloring evenly, keep drawing wet smooth lines. Note that chiaroscuro of leather material is stronger than that of cloth material, as shown in Fig.4.97 and Fig.4.98. Furthermore, some designers deliberately add the detailing effect of stitches when depicting leather material.

Fig.4.97 Leather egg chair

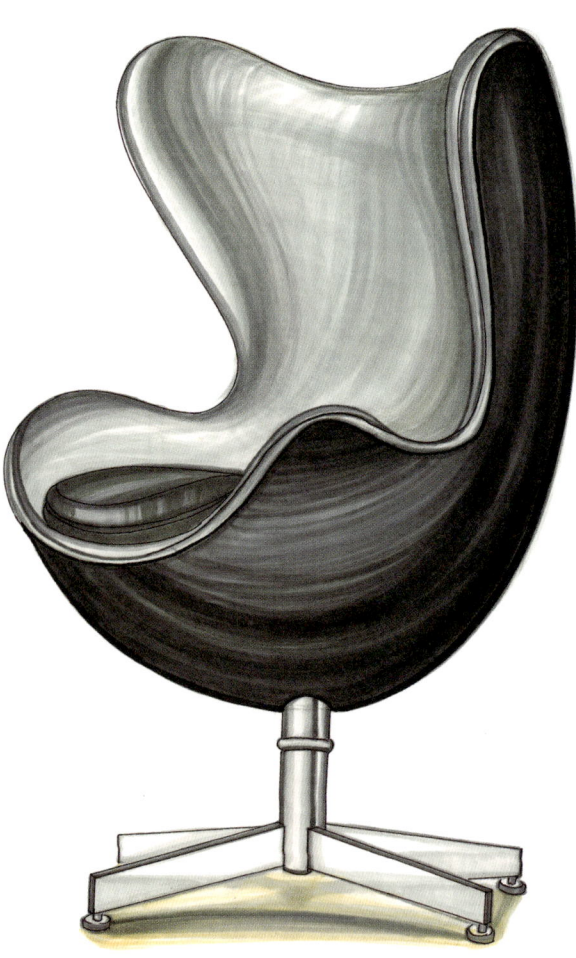

Fig.4.98 Detailing of leather egg chair done with marker pens

Now let's analyze the expression techniques of leather materials through an example of this leather chair, as shown in Fig.4.99.

Fig.4.99   Leather tiger chair

The shape of this leather tiger chair is a combination of squares and circles, with a bulging backrest, cylindrical armrests, and curving cylindrical supporting legs. Open design is the main characteristic of this chair. It's made of clean, sturdy and elastic leather. When representing it with marker pens, the smooth surface of the leather should be depicted. The color should be even and the chiaroscuro of leather should be stronger than that of the cloth material. You can use proper highlights and reflection to show the smoothness of leather. The specific steps are as follows.

Step 1: Draw an outline sketch of the sofa with clear and smooth lines, as shown in Fig.4.100.

Step 2: Use brown marker pens to show the dominant color of the sofa. In this step, one or two brown marker pens are usually required. It's best to take a dark one and a light one as this will make the tone more harmonious and won't make the picture dirty, messy and indistinct. Furthermore, the stroke should be smooth and thorough, without too much hesitation or casualness. Leave highlight areas before drawing and ensure the right direction of your marker pens strokes.

Fig.4.100   Outline sketch of the leather tiger chair

Expression Techniques of Product Material   101

You can overlay colors with your marker pens in the shadow line area a few more times if necessary, as shown in Fig.4.101.

Step 3: Accentuate chiaroscuro. Accentuating the chiaroscuro makes the body of the chair more stereoscopic. Use a unified tone, the chiaroscuro of highlight areas, shadow line areas and reflected light areas should be strictly demarcated. The scattered highlights depict the bulged in the backrest. Cover the entire area, and make sure all the bulges are even. Strokes should be orderly and smooth in the whole process. Try to use less crossed strokes, as shown in Fig.4.102.

Step 4: Refine details. Firstly, use a white highlight pen to draw the decorative details of metal nails and parts of highlight lines of the chair. Then use the black pencil for sketching in the details. Lastly, draw the cast shadow at the base of the chair to make the drawing more stereoscopic. In this way, the marker depiction of the single sofa is completed, as shown in Fig.4.103.

Fig.4.101 Color effect created using marker pens

Fig.4.102 Contrast details added

Fig.4.103 Finer details added

Technique of depicting hard non-reflective and opaque material

Hard, non-reflective, and lightproof material is mainly seen in wood, stone, crude pottery, and frosted plastic. It's characterized by even absorbency, no reflection and no photo-permeability. Some of these materials have a visible texture on the surface, as shown in Fig.4.104 to Fig.4.107.

In this section, we focus on depicting two materials with marker pens: wood and stone. The main characteristics of wood are the intrinsic color and wood texture. In general, wood is maize-yellow, light yellow, or brown, etc. So, in the expression with marker pens, the segments should be distinct, the structure should be clear, and the lines should be straight to highlight the texture. The contrast of light and shadow should be relatively inconspicuous, as shown in Fig.4.108 to Fig.4.110.

Fig.4.104 Wood

Fig.4.105 Stone

Fig.4.106 Pottery shard

Fig.4.107 Frosted plastic

Fig.4.108 Wood block

Fig.4.109 Wood blocks of various shapes

Fig.4.110 Sketch of wooden material using marker pens

Expression Techniques of Product Material

Fig.4.111 Wooden chair

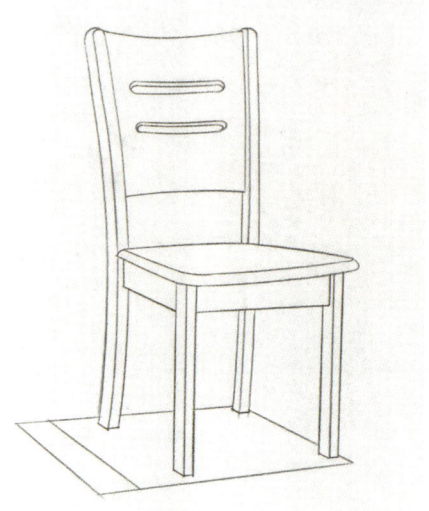

Fig.4.112 Outline sketch of the wooden chair

Now let's analyze the techniques of depicting wood surface through an example of this wooden chair, as shown in Fig.4.111. The specific steps are as follows.

Step 1: Draw an outline sketch of the wooden chair with clear and smooth lines, as shown in Fig.4.112.

Step 2: Use yellow marker pens to highlight the dominant color of the wodden chair and briefly distinguish the light and shade. When drawing the light side with marker pens, firstly pay attention to the direction of your marker pens as it decides the trend of wood grain. Secondly, the strokes should be gentle and fast. Leave white spaces as needed, as shown in Fig.4.113.

Step 3: Intensify chiaroscuro. In this step, accentuate the chiaroscuro to make the body of the chair more stereoscopic, as shown in Fig.4.114. Remember to keep the tone uniform and don't overlay with very contrasting colors.

Step 4: Add finer details. When you are drawing the wood texture of the chair with marker pens, control the direction and the strength of the strokes to depict the gradient of wood texture, but do not make it too obvious. A highlight pen and black pencil can also be used to add details. The last step is to draw the cast shadow at the base of the chair. In this way, depicting the wooden chair using markers is completed, as shown in Fig.4.115.

Fig.4.113 Color effect created with marker pens

Fig.4.114 Contrast details added

Similar to wood, the main features of stone are its intrinsic color, texture, and surface markings. In general, stone is maize-yellow, taupe or cyan, brown etc. So when depicting this surface with marker pens, the segments should be distinct, the structure should be clear, and the lines should be straight. You can additionally draw the surface markings and highlight the texture using moderate chiaroscuro and shading.

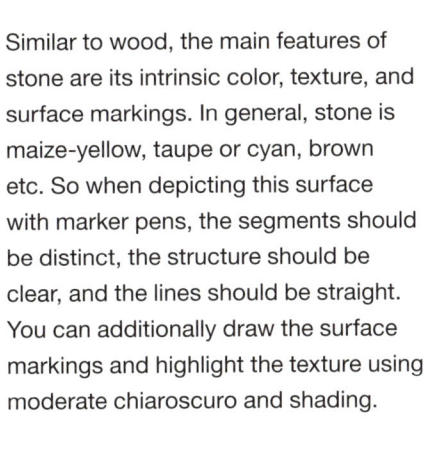

Fig.4.115 Finer details added in the sketch

Expression Techniques of Product Material   **107**

Now let's make a specific analysis of the techniques of depicting stone materials through the example of outdoor bench, as shown in Fig.4.116.

Firstly, the shape of this outdoor bench is very simple, basically made up of incisal corner cuboid and banding cuboid. Secondly, the outdoor bench is made of wood and stone. When using marker pens to draw this bench, you need to distinguish the difference of characteristics of these two materials, including the intrinsic colors of wood, the texture and the inherent color of stone and the lithosporic effect. The specific steps are as follows.

Fig.4.116 Outdoor bench

Step 1: Draw an outline sketch of the bench with clear and smooth lines, as shown in Fig.4.117.

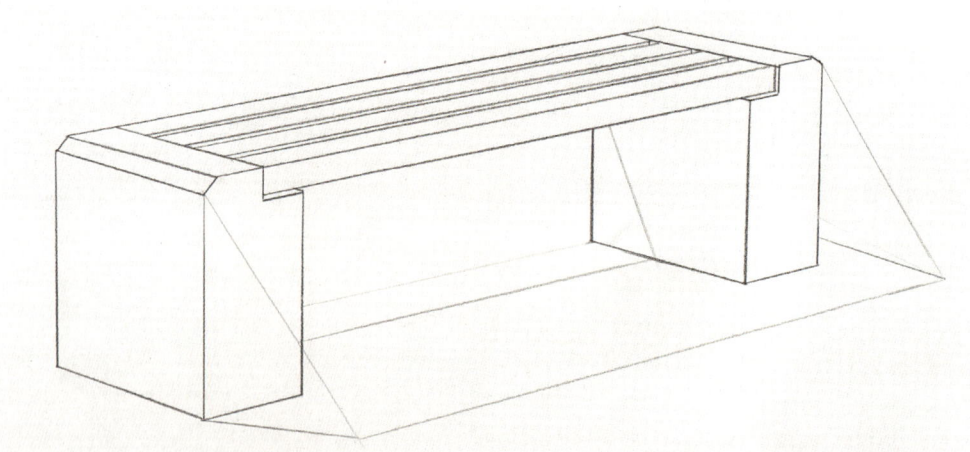

Fig.4.117 Outline sketch of the outdoor bench

Step 2: Use yellow marker pens to show the wood texture of this bench. Briefly distinguish the light and shade to represent the wood texture, as shown in Fig.4.118.

Step 3: Use gray marker pens to show the stone texture of this bench. Distinguish the light and shade relations. Use orderly strokes of the marker pens to make the segments distinct, as shown in Fig.4.119.

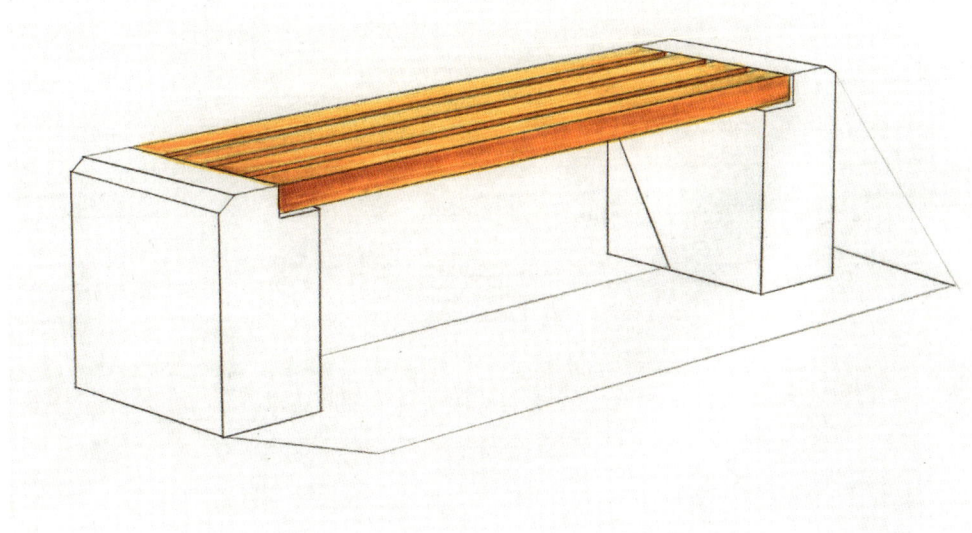

Fig.4.118 Detailing the wooden surface using marker pens

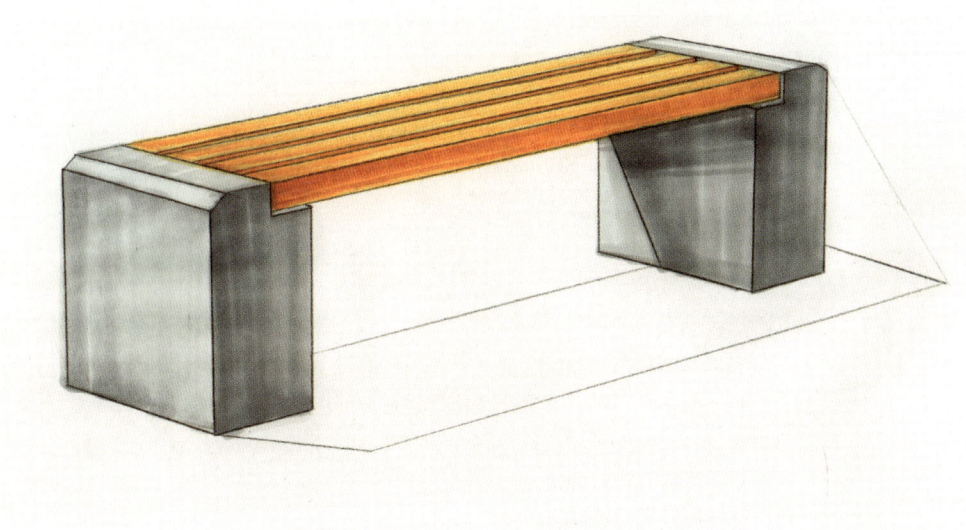

Fig.4.119 Creating light and shade effect on the stone using marker pens

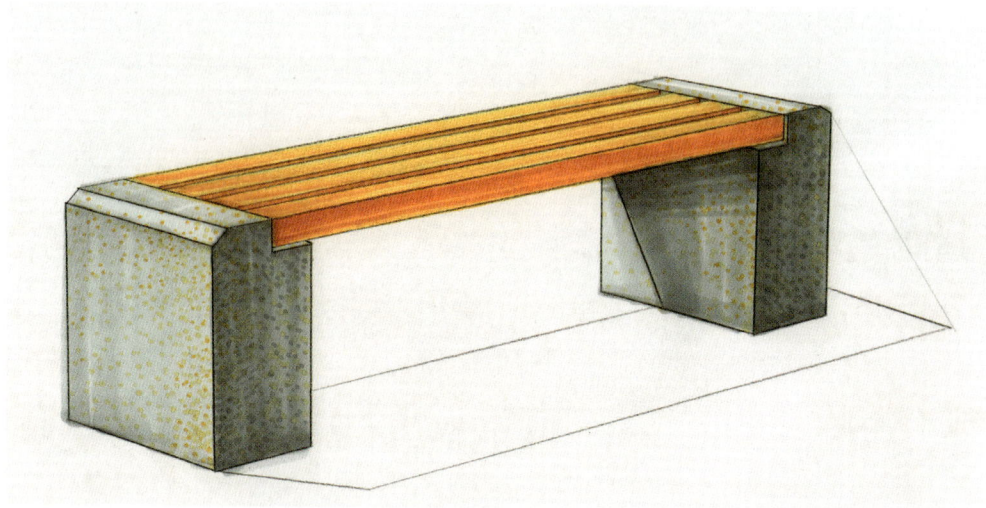

Fig.4.120 Detailing the stone surface using marker pens

Step 4: Use gray and yellow marker pens to show the stone texture of this bench. The specific technique here is to use the nib of the marker pens to make dots. The strokes should vary in weight and density and not be too neat , to keep the drawing natural and harmonious. Do not use more than three kinds of colors, as shown in Fig.4.120.

Step 5: Draw the details and draw the cast shadow. A highlighter can be used to increase brightness of details. The cast shadow should not be too dark. Exaggerate shading changes to improve the transparency of the picture and make it more beautiful, as shown in Fig.4.121.

Fig.4.121 Finer details including shadow created using marker pens

Material Expression with Marker Pens

When you use marker pens to depict materials or textures, keep these points in mind:

1. Use of strokes
For most materials, coloring with markers should be steady and fast without any hesitation. The direction of the stroke depends on the direction of modeling, the shadow line, edges, and so on. If you can't finish a stroke, you need to pick it up before the ink is dry. Use strokes that vary in thickness, direction, density, and length.

2. Color selection
When using marker pens to color, it's good to use one hue as the dominant tone. The inherent color should be clear and definite, and then match it with other two or three colors. Be sure to keep in mind that you do not use too many kinds of colors, preferably do not use more than three. Furthermore, the coloring order with marker pens should be from light to dark. You can leave white spaces moderately within the highlight part and the reflected light part.

3. Knowledge and innovation
Expression techniques with marker pens need a lot of practise, more knowledge and more innovations. The methods and skills in this book can be acquired through continuous practises, and can be used as reference in future study. Our work has many deficiencies. It is important to keep learning and innovating by starting from products with a simple structure and single material, and then increasing the difficulty step by step to cultivate our own interest and confidence and persevering with it. We believe that in this way, we can do well in the expression of various materials.

Instance Analysis of Product Modeling Design

CHAPTER 5

Instance Analysis of Product Design for Computer and Accessories

Computer and accessory products include desktop computers, laptop computers, keyboards, mouse, USB flash drives, mobile HDD, external webcams, game controls, printers, copiers, monitors, scanners, optical lanterns, projectors, wireless routers, etc.

Portable micro-projector design

To design a portable micro-projector, we need to figure out the common models of projectors available in the market, which projectors are portable, and what are the design features.

As shown in Fig.5.1 to Fig.5.6, at present, there are various types of projectors in the market, including many conveniently sized projectors, with various shapes such as rectangle, circle, ellipse, cylinder.
The structural designs mainly include scaffolding type, retractable type, rotary type, folding type, etc.

After familiarizing ourselves with the various projector models in the market, we need to understand the structures of these projectors

Fig.5.1 Rectangular box projector

Fig.5.2 Curved scaffolding projector

Fig.5.3 Circular shrinking projector

Fig.5.4 Circular rotary projector

Fig.5.5 Cylindrical folding projector

Fig.5.6 Cylindrical projector

and analyze morphological features. We can think about the basic structure of products in our daily life and extract their geometric solids including folded structure, scissor structure, cutting structure and telescoping structure, etc. These structures, are highly contractile, which can enhance the convenience and storage of the projector, as shown in Fig.5.7 to Fig.5.10.

A comparison of these structures shows that while the folding structure has a good storage function, its supporting structure is relatively complex; the cutting structure is easy to expand and close but is not conducive to adjusting direction; and while the telescoping structure has the best performance in terms of concealment, is convenient to receive and is dust-proof, it's not easy to carry. Hence, the scissor structure is the best choice as it's adjustable and easy to carry. Now let's analyze the geometric structure of the projector, as shown in Fig.5.11.

Instance Analysis of Product Modeling Design

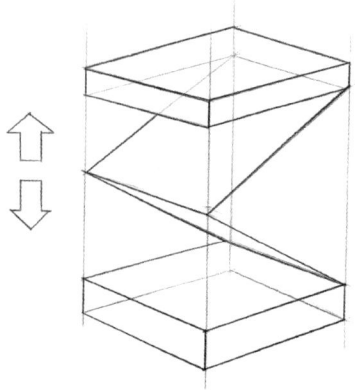

Fig.5.7 Foldable structure

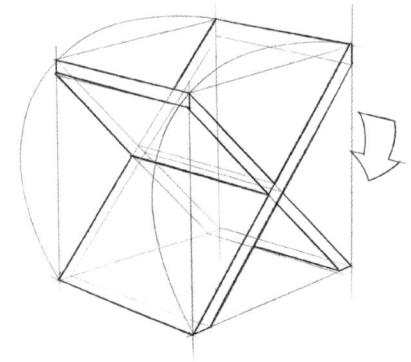

Fig.5.8 Scissor structure

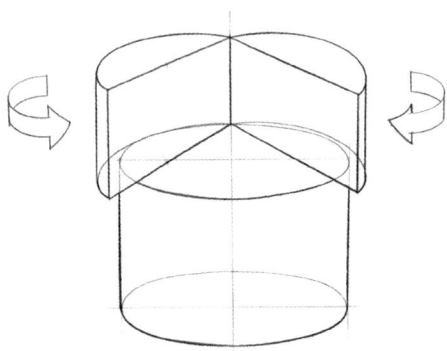

Fig.5.9 Cutting structure

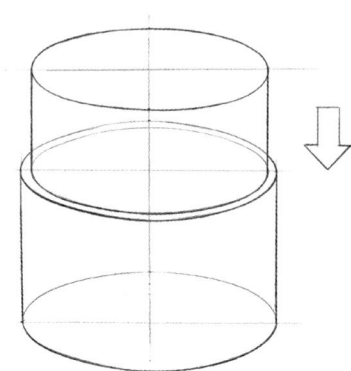

Fig.5.10 Telescoping structure

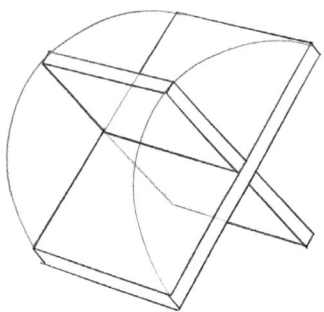
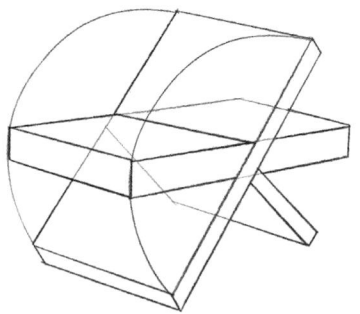

Fig.5.11 Analysis of projector geometry

We can determine the storage mode of the projector by analyzing its structure. Then we focus on the necessary components, materials, basic requirements, and functions of projectors, including lens, buttons, ports, handle and other details. Then, we draw a draft design, as shown in Fig.5.12.

Once the draft design scheme is completed, the modeling design is finalized. Then we can move on to the next stage: depicting the material with marker pens. This portable projector is made of three materials: plastic material for the main body of the device, metal surface of the scissor structure, and textile material used in the handle strap. Now, we use marker pens to depict the materials of this portable projector. Specific steps are as follows.

Step 1: Draw an outline sketch of the projector, as shown in Fig.5.13. You can recompose and represent it with clear and smooth lines in accordance with the draft design. Then, add the background and the shape of the projector when it is closed, based on the draft. Tilt the final product image (on the right) towards the left to make the image more vivid.

Step 2: Use blue marker pens to depict the plastic material of the projector. The blue plastic part of the projector includes the host panel and the inner side of the support frame. Use the marker pens to highlight the blue, try not to add other colors. In this case, two blue marker pens, one light and one dark, are used to widen the color hierarchy and keep the strokes smooth. For the bulge on the host panel, leave a white space to show the curved surface, as shown in Fig.5.14.

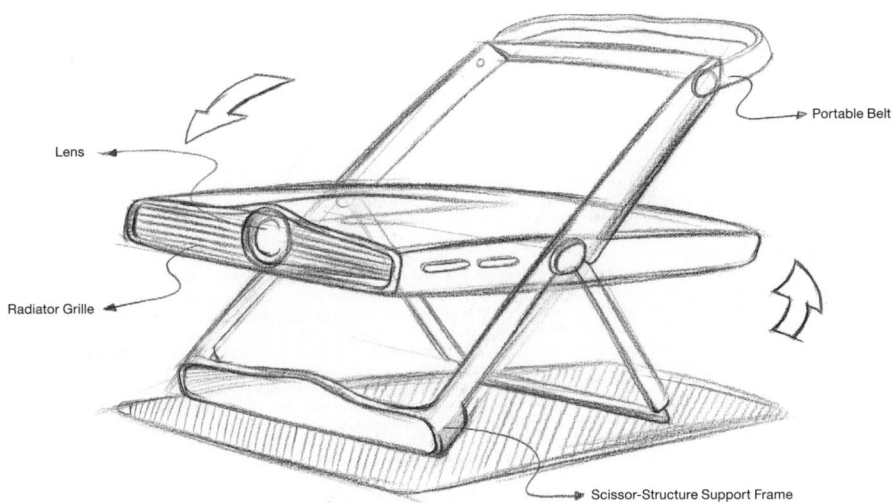

Fig.5.12 Design draft of portable projector

Instance Analysis of Product Modeling Design

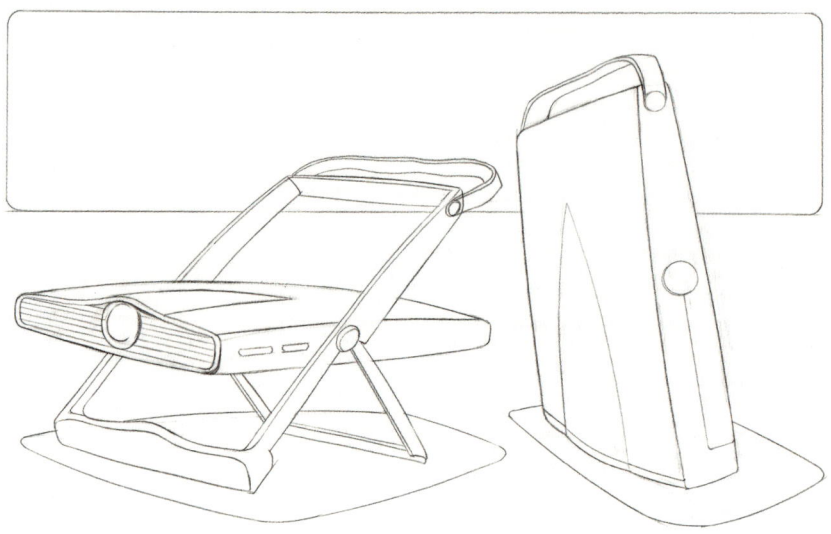

Fig.5.13   Outline sketch of the portable projector

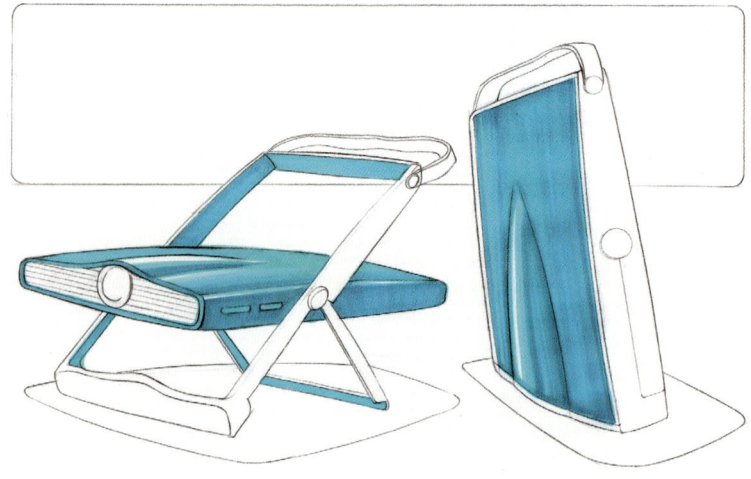

Fig.5.14   Impression of blue plastic texture created with marker pens

Step 3: Use gray marker pens to depict the metal material of the projector. The metal parts are the outer frame of the scissor structure and the two round fasteners. Deepen the tone of the product to give the impression of weight, as shown in Fig.5.15.

Step 4: Use gray and yellow marker pens to draw the lens and handle of the projector. Firstly, draw the lens of the projector, including the radiator grille and the photoflood lamp. The photoflood lamp made of convex glass material is highly reflective. The radiator grille is a striated structure, so it can be represented by a contrast of two gray color layers. Secondly, the handle is made of soft fabric. It can be presented by soft lines and neutral colors, as shown in Fig.5.16.

Step 5: Refine details. First use a black pencil and a white highlighter to depict details and highlights, respectively, to add the finer details to the picture. Then, draw the background and cast shadow of the projector to make the whole picture more stereoscopic and give a sense of space. The last step is to complete the drawing of the portable projector, as shown in Fig.5.17.

The design of the portable projector shows us how we can analyze and design products well, using the perspective of structure and shape. Of course, there are many ways to design products. Remember that working on every design is a good experience. We need to constantly forge ahead to improve ourselves in the road to design.

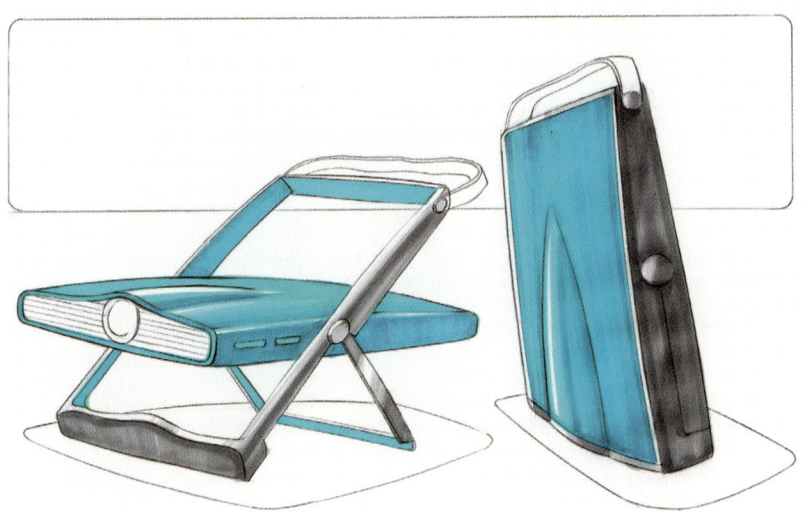

Fig.5.15 Metallic surface detailing done with marker pens

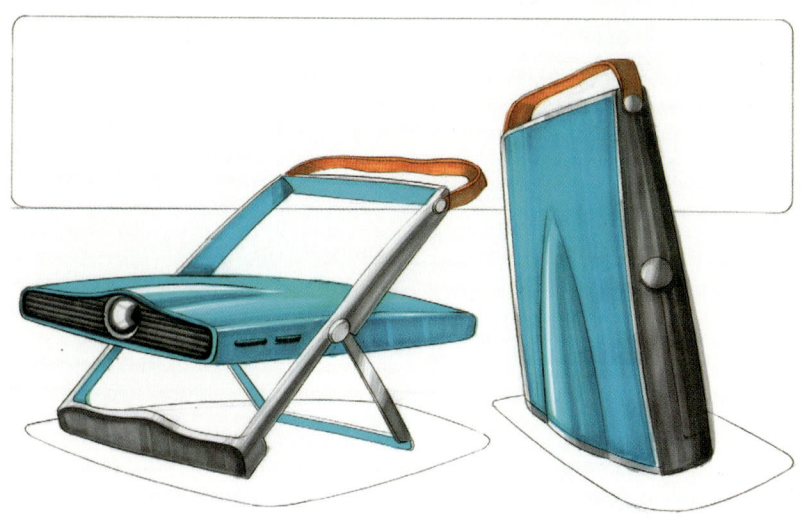

Fig.5.16 Details of lens surface and handle drawn using marker pens

Fig.5.17 Finer details added

Instance Analysis of Product Design for Office Furniture

Office furniture products include office desks and chairs, conference room tables and chairs, filing cabinets, stationery and recreational products, etc. This type of product is intended for use in specific locations, such as companies, industries, and campuses. These products are commonly made of leather, wood, metal, plastic, etc. In this section, we learn about designs for these products through an instance analysis.

Computer chair design

Computers are indispensable for our work, study, entertainment and other needs, but they also have adverse effects on the body. Sitting and using a computer for a long time can affect the neck, shoulders, spine, lumbar joints, and other parts. An ergonomically designed computer chair, as shown in Fig.5.18 to Fig.5.21, can ensure proper posture, alleviate physical fatigue and prevent damage to a certain extent. In this chapter, we are going to design a computer chair for office, study, entertainment, and relaxation.

Fig.5.18　Sitting position (1)

Fig.5.19　Sitting position (2)

Instance Analysis of Product Modeling Design

Fig.5.20 Reclining

Fig.5.21 Lying flat

As shown in Fig.5.22 to Fig.5.29, there are several types of computer chairs currently in the market, including split type, integrated type, reclining type, flat lying type, etc. to meet the needs of different groups of people. The split computer chair can be split or closed; it is expensive but utilizes less space. The integrated computer chair solves the problem of computer placement during work, leisure, and entertainment. However, it is inconvenient to adjust the sitting angle and it cannot be used to lie flat. Reclining and flat lying computer chairs can help adjust the sitting posture better and can also serve as temporary beds, but they are not easy to store.

Fig.5.22 Split computer chair (1)

Fig.5.23 Split computer chair (2)

Fig.5.24 Integrated computer chair (1)

Fig.5.25 Integrated computer chair (2)

Fig.5.26 Reclining computer chair (1)

Fig.5.27 Reclining computer chair (2)

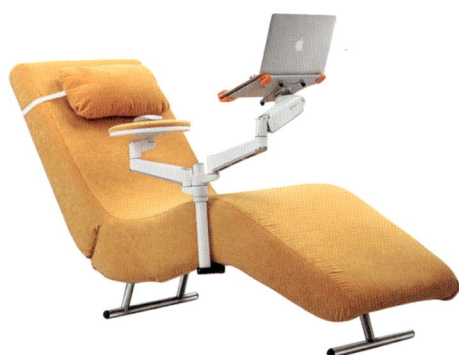
Fig.5.28 Flat lying computer chair (1)

Fig.5.29 Flat lying computer chair (2)

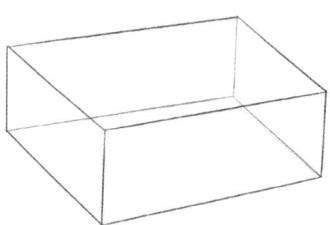

Fig.5.30 Structure of carton (1)

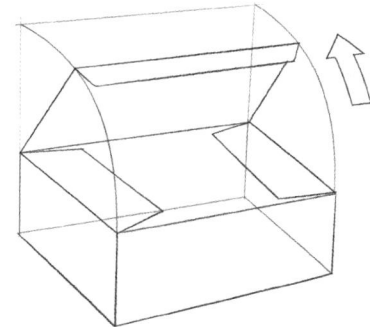

Fig.5.31 Structure of carton (2)

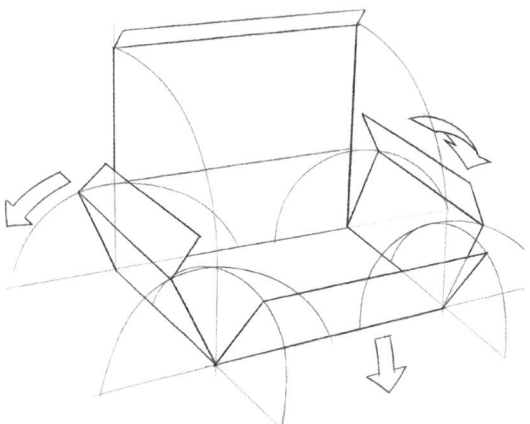

Fig.5.32 Structure of carton (3)

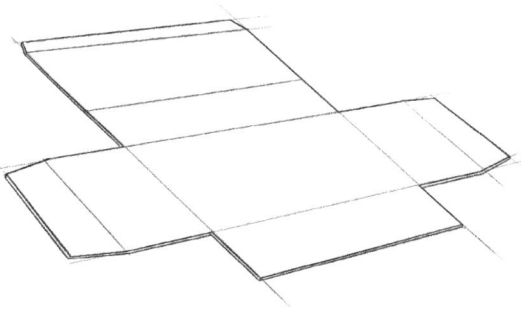

Fig.5.33 Structure of carton (4)

Through the comparison and analysis of various computer chairs available in the market, we find that to design a computer chair for work, study, entertainment and rest, it must have an optimal structure that not only meets the functional requirements, but also should be easy to store. The design should be reasonable and practical with simple and reliable structure. We analyze the geometric solid of the computer chair using the basic structure of a carton structure, as shown in Fig.5.30 to Fig.5.33. The carton has a simple and firm structure and is convenient to fold.

The design direction of the computer chair is basically determined by analyzing the geometric structure of the carton. Then, the corresponding design draft is made based on the modeling and the structure of the computer chair, as shown in Fig.5.34 to Fig.5.35.

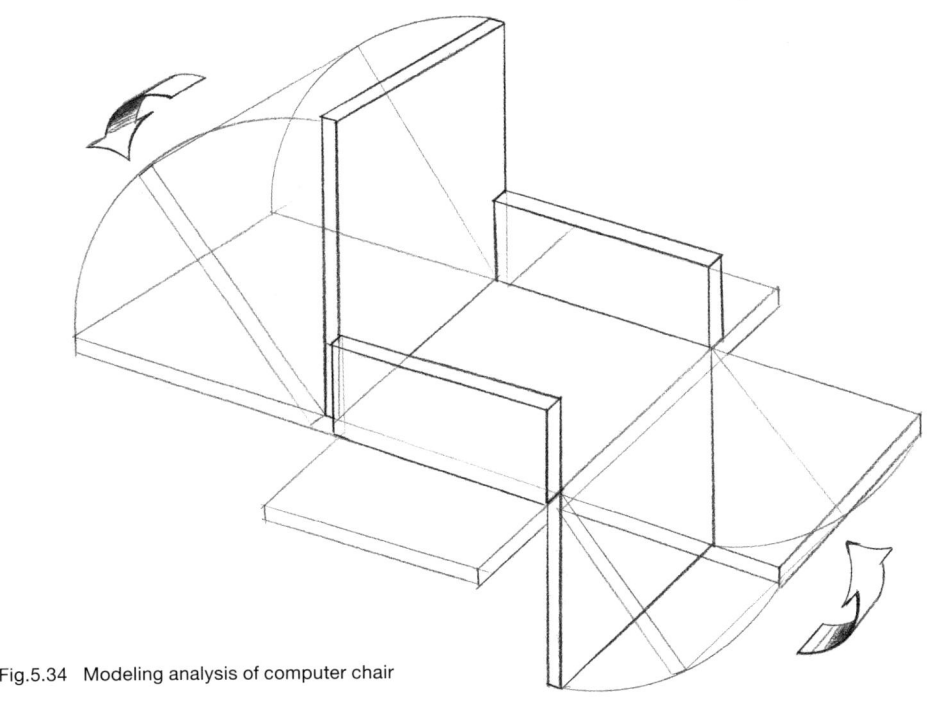

Fig.5.34　Modeling analysis of computer chair

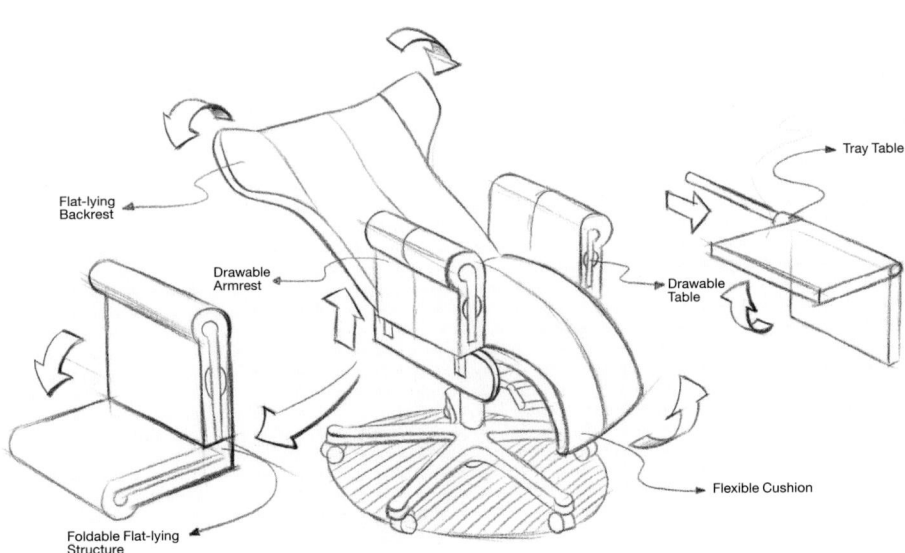

Fig.5.35　A sketch of the computer chair

After completing the design sketch, we have a clearer idea about the modeling design of the computer chair, and then we complete the final detailing. As the unfolding structure of the computer chair is a bit complicated, the unfolding process needs to be clearly depicted. So before drawing with marker pens, first of all, the sketch must be re-composed and the view of the chair in the unfolded state, detailed analysis, and structural description must be added. Secondly, it is necessary to determine the material used for the computer chair, including leather materials, wood materials, and metal materials. The specific steps are as follows.

Step 1: Draw an outline sketch of the computer chair. Recompose the picture in line with the previous design sketch, and add several diagrams showing the chair in the unfolded state and its structural analysis. Use simple and smooth lines to present the model of the computer chair, as shown in Fig.5.36.

Step 2: Use gray marker pens to depict the leather material of the computer chair. Leather material is mainly used in the back, cushion, and armrest of the computer chair. Keep the strokes of the markers fluent to emphasize the smoothness of the leather. Don't leave too much white space in the highlight area, and ensure there are

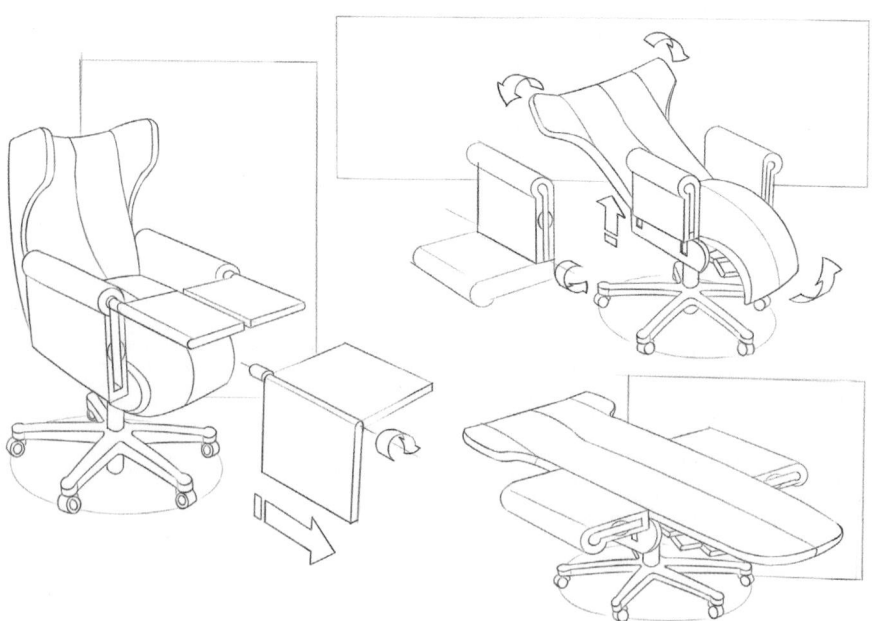

Fig.5.36 Outline sketch of the computer chair

gradations of dark colors. It is important to control the overall direction of the stroke, as shown in Fig.5.37.

Step 3: Use yellow marker pens to depict the wooden surface of the computer desk. It is important to express the intrinsic color and highlight the texture of wood at the same time. Pay attention to the direction of strokes and the chiaroscuro effect, as shown in Fig.5.38.

Step 4: Use gray marker pens to depict the metal and plastic materials of the computer chair chassis. The chassis includes a metal base stand and several plastic castors. Try to achieve a reflective and glossy effect with markers when depicting the metal base stand. When depicting plastic castors, as the castors are relatively small, try to keep the sketch simple and coordinate the overall colors, as shown in Fig.5.39.

Step 5: Complete the design. First, use arrows to indicate the steps in the analysis of the unfolded state, to better show the various structures of the computer chair. Then, use the highlighter to show the stitches in the leather. Finally, draw the background of the computer chair and the cast shadow to make the picture complete and three-dimensional. Fig.5.40, shows the complete design of a computer chair that can be used for office use, study, entertainment, and rest.

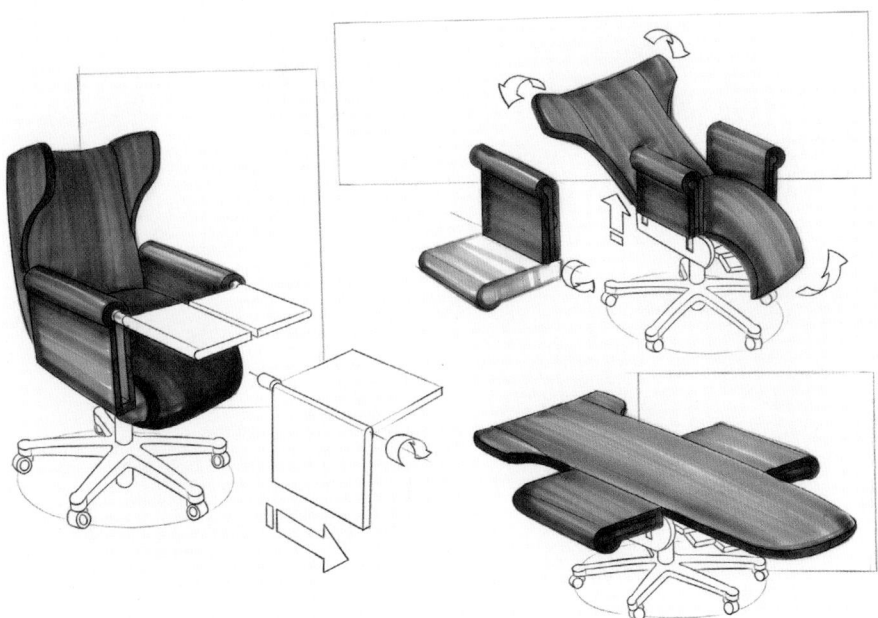

Fig.5.37 Leather texture created using marker pens

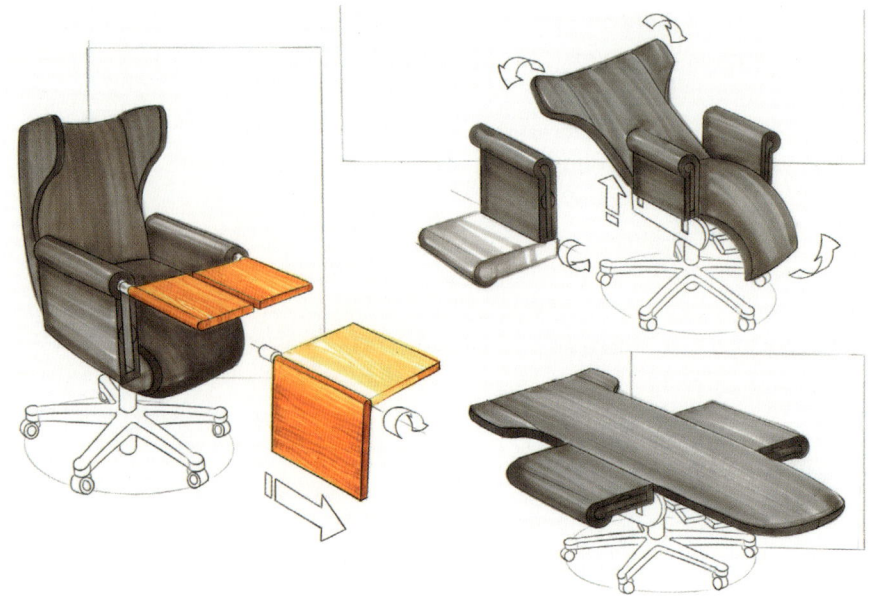

Fig.5.38 Wooden surface texture created using marker pens

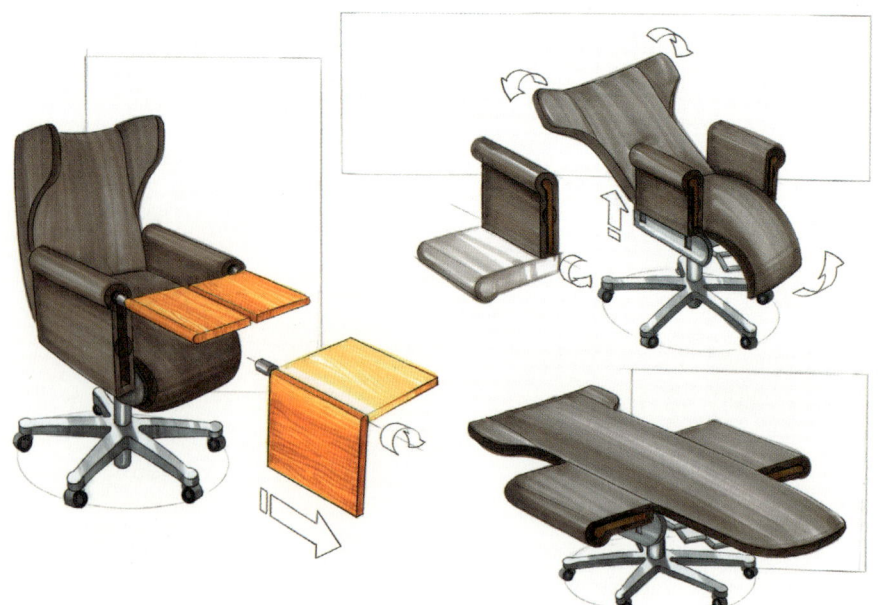

Fig.5.39 Adding the swivel section details using marker pens

In this design study, we cover the functional requirements and the structure of the product, compare advantages of various computer chair types, and finally design a multi-functional computer chair. This case helps us to train our creativity in design, enhances our understanding of product structure design, and at the same time builds our skills to depict a variety of materials with marker pens.

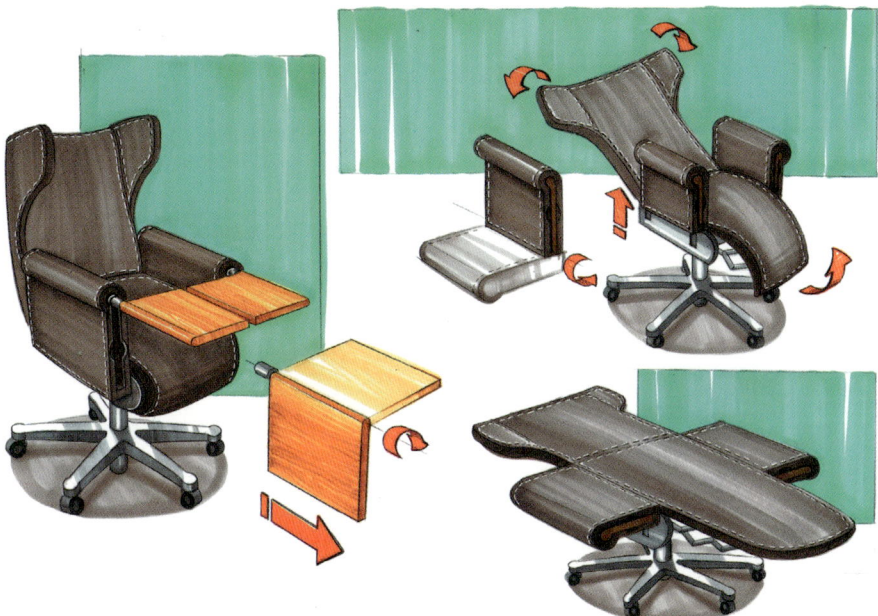

Fig.5.40 The completed design sketch

Instance Analysis of Product Design for Lighting Products

Lighting products include indoor and outdoor lighting fixtures and their accessories. The common ones are spotlights, wall lamps, ground lamps, ceiling lamps, table lamps, floor lamps, trail lamps, landscape lamps, flashlights, etc. Such products generally include light sources, reflector plates, fixtures, and other parts. Materials such as glass, plastic, metal, etc. are mainly used. Of course, the highlights of this type of product lie in the rich modeling features and the unique light and shadow effect of each design.

Path lights design

The path light is a kind of lamp used for ground lighting in public places such as outdoor squares, parks, green spaces, and sidewalks. Path lights are available in a variety of practical and attractive designs for brilliant night lighting effects, as shown in Fig.5.41 to Fig.5.48.

Fig.5.41   Park path light (1)

Fig.5.42   Park path light (2)

Fig.5.43 Path light in a rest area (1)

Fig.5.44 Path light in a rest area (2)

Fig.5.45 Sidewalk path light (1)

Fig.5.46 Sidewalk path light (2)

Fig.5.47 Solar path light (1)

Fig.5.48 Solar path light (2)

Instance Analysis of Product Modeling Design

Fig.5.49 Coconut tree (1)

Fig.5.50 Coconut tree (2)

In this section, we are going to design a multi-purpose path light. Before designing, we need to consider several aspects in the design of path lights:

First, safety is the top priority in road lighting design, and path lights must pose no threat to personal safety.

Second, the design of the path lights must meet the functional requirements of road lighting, which can be measured by some criteria, such as the power and lumen value of the light source.

Third, the design of path lights should add to the sense of beauty of the environmental landscape. We cannot overlook aesthetic requirements and need a design that will blend in. For this, we integrate local cultural elements into the design and continue to add value by creating cultural brands.

Fourth, cost issues. We must factor in various aspects such as the manufacturing costs, molds, assembly, construction, installation, and the convenience of later maintenance when considering the cost of the product. The designed path lights must be capable of being mass-produced through modularization and are not meant to be sculptures.

Fifth, traditionally, outdoor lights are designed only to meet the lighting needs with little attention to appearance. These are now available in modern styles and are energy efficient. The internet has also contributed to achieve a multi-purpose design, bringing more convenience into people's daily life.

To sum up, to design a multi-function path light, we must not only ensure its safety and practicality, but also consider the aesthetics, intelligence, and environmental protection. Firstly, the path light should have a reasonable and safe structure and convenient operation; secondly, the design should appear aesthetic and concise, and finally, it must be a high-tech product with great added value.

Fig.5.51 Bionic design of path light

We can proceed with the specific plan design after determining the design positioning. As the structure of the path light is relatively simple, we start from the modeling design and adopt the bionic design. Bionic design takes the shape, color, sound, function and structure of objects in nature as the research subjects and applies these characteristics in the design process. It brings new ideas, new principles and new ways to modeling design.

In this case, the bionic design is based on coconut trees. Through the deduction of the shape of the coconut tree, we gradually get the shape of the path lights we want, as shown in Fig.5.49 to Fig.5.51.

We determine the basic modeling characteristics of the path lights through deduction and analysis of the bionic structure. Next, we design the function, structure, materials, and details of the path lights, and draw an outline sketch of the design, as shown in Fig.5.52.

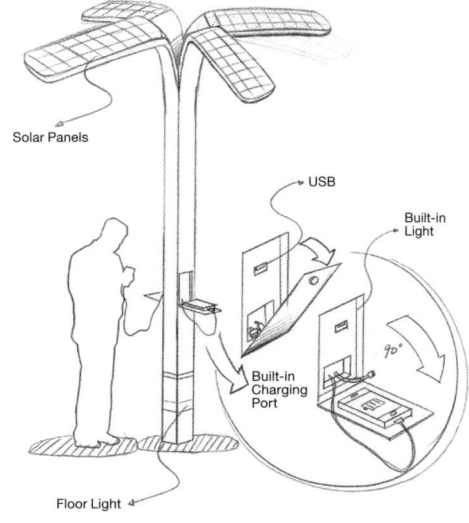

Fig.5.52 Sketch of the design scheme of the path light

As per the design sketch, firstly, we decide the material of the path light. The material is mainly composed of mirror solar panels, stainless steel lamp posts, and transparent lampshades. Secondly, we recompose the picture and draw the modeling outline draft. Then, we use marker pens to present

Instance Analysis of Product Modeling Design 133

material of the path lights in order, and complete the final rendering. The specific steps are as follows.

Step 1: Draw a sketch. Recompose the picture based on the sketch, express the local structure through the detailed drawing, and finally express the modeling sketch of the path light with simple and smooth lines, as shown in Fig.5.53.

Step 2: Use marker pens to depict the mirror material of the solar panel. We haved used blue marker pen to draw hatchings to express the delicate, smooth, and highly reflective surface of the mirror material. The strokes should be smooth, the gradations of light and shade should be general, and white space must be left appropriately within the highlight part, as shown in Fig.5.54.

Step 3: Use a marker pen to depict the metal material of the lamp post. Use gray marker pens to present the metal material of the lamp post in order. Due to the flat metal part of the lamp post, the stroke should be tiled to maintain the overall flatness, and the contrast is mainly emphasized in the curved part. In addition, the stroke should also reflect the appropriate gradient effect, as shown in Fig.5.55.

Fig.5.53　Outline sketch

Fig.5.54　Details of solar panel created with marker pens

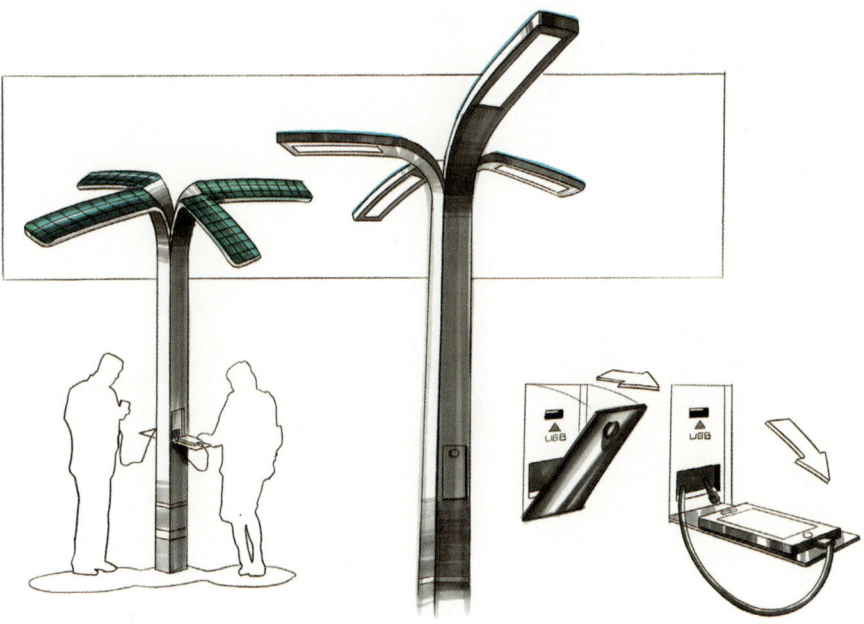

Fig.5.55　Details of lamp post created with marker pens

Step 4: Use marker pen to show the lighting effect. Using yellow marker pens can not only show the bright light from the bulb, but also the light and shadow effect of the built-in light when the charging port is turned on. When using a marker pen to express light, you must control the direction and intensity of the stroke. The stroke should not be too dense, and the color should not be too dark. It is best to be able to vaguely see the objects behind, reflecting the light permeability, as shown in Fig.5.56.

Step 5: Refine details. Firstly, we can provide a reference for the design of path lights through character modeling and scene close-ups. Secondly, the reconstruction and further explanation through detailed drafts can better reflect the multi-functional purpose of the light. Then, draw the background and cast shadow of the path light to complete the design of the multi-functional path light, as shown in Fig.5.57.

Fig.5.56 Details of lighting effect created with marker pens

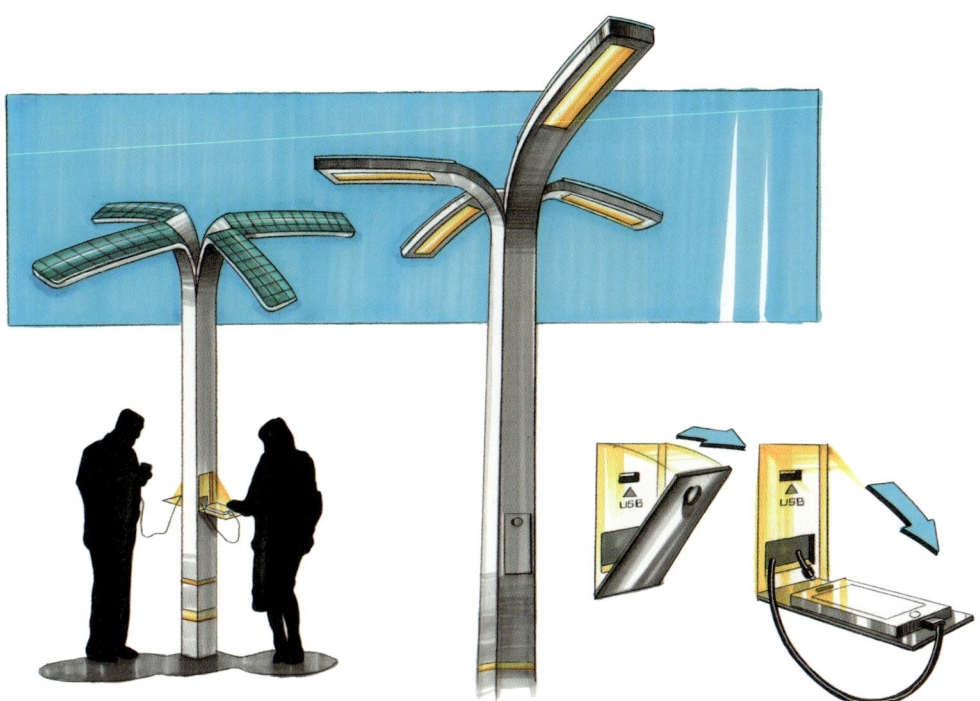

Fig.5.57　The completed design sketch

Instance Analysis of Product Design for Home and Living Products

Home and living products include home appliances, kitchen items, tableware, sanitary, and bathroom equipment, home decoration and accessories, etc. Home appliances refer to household appliances, divided into white goods and brown goods. White goods are products that can help people do routine housekeeping tasks or improve the living environment and living standards, such as washing machines, rice cookers, refrigerators, and air conditioners. Brown goods are products that provide entertainment, such as color TVs, stereos, and game consoles. Kitchen items are appliances used in the kitchen and mainly including range hoods, gas stoves, pots, knives, etc. Tableware includes bowls, chopsticks, plates, basins, plates, spoons, cups, etc. Sanitary and bathroom equipment include sink, bidet, faucet, shower, bathtub, etc. Home decoration accessories include all kinds of furniture, and smaller decorative objects. Most of the household life products are made of plastics, metals, ceramics, etc., and have some typical features such as simplicity of use, human utility, and creativity.

Tableware design

Tableware refers to utensils used to aid in food preparation, presentation, and consumption. At present, there are metal tableware, ceramic tableware, tea sets, wine vessels, glassware, paper utensils, and plastic utensils in the market. Containers of bowls, plates, cups, and pots, as well as chopsticks, knives, forks, spoons, straws, and sticks are also included, as shown in Fig.5.58 to Fig.5.63.

Fig.5.58　Ceramic tableware

Fig.5.59　Metal tableware

Fig.5.60　Glass tea set

Fig.5.61 Plastic utensils   Fig.5.62 Disposable paper utensils   Fig.5.63 Disposable plastic tableware

With the progress of society and the development of material life, people pay increasing amount of attention to the environment of family life and the quality of life. Choosing an appropriate family tableware set not only enhances the style of the home and ambiance of the restaurant, but also lights up the mood and increases appetite when people are eating.

This section focuses on the design of a set of tableware representing national cultural features. The chosen material of the tableware is ceramics, and the blue and white porcelain is the design pattern adopted, and then the final renderings are drawn. The specific steps are as follows.

Step 1: Draw a modeling sketch. Draw the final modeling outline rendering in line with the design plan, as shown in Fig.5.64.

Step 2: Use gray marker pens to express the background color of the ceramic material. The ceramic material has a smooth surface and fine texture, giving people a gentle and soft impression. The overall tone of the teapot is in neutral colors and has neither elaborate chiaroscuro nor flamboyant tint. For this reason, off-white is a good tone to choose when you use marker pens. You can use gray markers to color a large area. Don't forget to leave white space in highlight areas. Don't make the shadow line areas too obvious and draw the gradients carefully, as shown in Fig.5.65.

Step 3: Intensify chiaroscuro and create the gradient effect. Highlight the texture of ceramic materials, which is specifically reflected in the high finish, the white space in the highlight area, the gradient of the transition between the highlight area and the shadow line area, and the slight dark shadow area. This gives the product an elegant stereoscopic effect, as shown in Fig.5.66.

Step 4: Add the blue and white pattern. Use a blue marker pen to draw the blue and white pattern on the surface of the tableware. In this step, use strokes of the same thickness. The strokes in the highlight area can be lighter, and heavier in the dark area, so that the effect of light and shadow changes can be well reflected, as shown in Fig.5.67.

Fig.5.64 Outline sketch

Fig.5.65 Detailing the background color with marker pens

Fig.5.66 Chiaroscuro detailing

Fig.5.67 Blue and white pattern detailing added

Step 5: Refine details. Draw the background and the cast shadow of the tableware. In principle, the background is to offset the main product, so the color should not be too similar to the main product, so as not to cause confusion. Moreover, as ceramic products are basically white, using dark gray to express the cast shadow can highlight the ceramic texture and make the overall picture more stable and three-dimensional. Finally, complete the tableware design with ethnic elements and the marker rendering, as shown in Fig.5.68.

Fig.5.68 The completed design sketch

Instance Analysis of Product Design for Industrial and Construction Facilities

Industrial and construction facility products include production equipment, power tools, factory facilities, measuring tools, sanitary equipment, production machines, processing facilities, windows, doors, balconies, awnings, handrails, roofs, greenhouses, garages, solar energy equipment, and fireplaces, etc. This type of product is mainly functional, with ingenious design and complicated manufacturing process.

Power tools design

In 1895, the first DC electric drill was developed in Germany, beginning the era of power tools for human use. For more than 120 years, power tools have grown from scratch, from elementary to advanced, and have now formed three major product series: industrial production, maintenance applications, and home assistance. There are hundreds of varieties, thousands of specifications, and an annual output of more than 8 million units. The modern power tool has become an indispensable tool for human production, work and daily life. Especially over the past 10 years, with the development of electronic technology, various electronic control technologies have been used in power tools, which not only promotes the performance of the tools, but also improves the processing quality, flexibility, and product added value. This has pushsed the power tool to a new stage of rapid development of mechatronics.

Power tools are divided into cutting power tools, grinding power tools, and assembling power tools. Common power tools include electric cutters, electric grinders, electric saws, electric planers, electric drills, electric hammers, electric wrenches, electric screwdrivers, concrete vibrators, etc., as shown in Fig.5.69 to Fig.5.76.

Fig.5.69 Chainsaw

Fig.5.70 Jigsaw

Fig.5.71 Miter saw

Fig.5.72 Circular saw

Fig.5.73 Angle grinder

Fig.5.74 Planer

Fig.5.75 Electric drill

Fig.5.76 Impact electric drill

Electric tools have comprehensive functions and are available in a wide range of types. However, the complicated structures and large toolboxes make them hard to store and carry. To address this problem, in this section we design a foldable and portable electric drill that is easy to carry.

First, we look at the scheme design. The design concept of the helmet originates from the hedgehog. The hard semi-circular structure of the helmet is just like the hedgehog curled into a ball when defending itself. Together, they constitute the shape element of the electric drill when it is folded. The bionic deduction of the modeling structure can be extracted to the design plan of the electric drill, as shown in Fig.5.77.

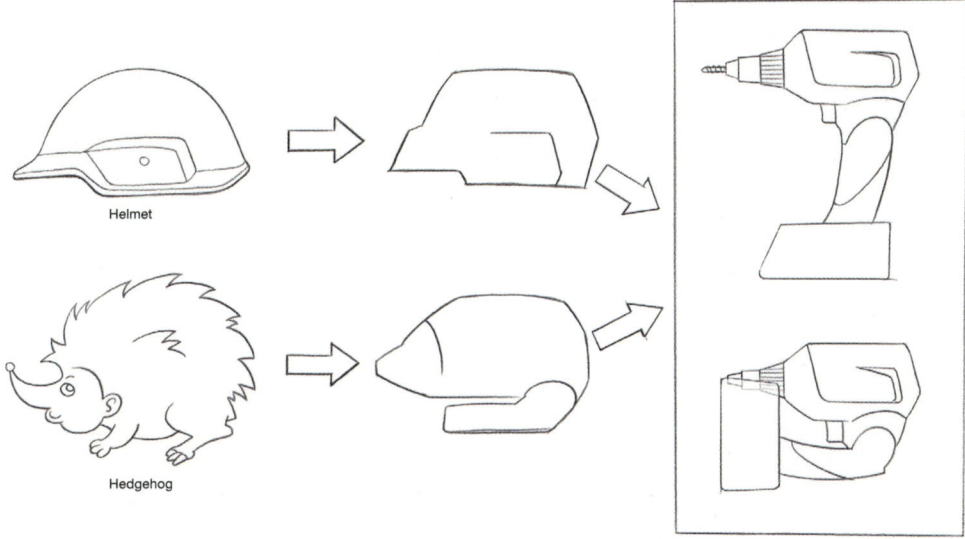

Fig.5.77 Modeling bionic deduction

Instance Analysis of Product Modeling Design

Next, refine the function, structure, materials, and details of the drill in detail, and draw a sketch of the design, as shown in Fig.5.78.

The sketch design shows that the material of the foldable and portable electric drill is mainly metal and plastic. Next, draw the final renderings. The specific steps are as follows.

Step 1: Draw a modeling sketch. The final rendering is drawn based on the sketch, in which the background of the product highlights the segments, and the two states of the electric drill are coordinated and merged. Draw the modeling sketch of the electric drill with clear and smooth lines, as shown in Fig.5.79.

Step 2: Use marker pens to express the metal material of the electric drill. Use gray marker pens to express the metal texture of the electric drill in turn, and control the overall tone. Don't cover fully with too many strokes. It is also necessary to maintain the smoothness and unity of the picture, and to highlight the contrast of metal, as shown in Fig.5.80.

Step 3: Use marker pens to depict the yellow plastic material of the electric drill. The plastic part of the electric drill includes yellow and black parts, and the surface of the plastic material is delicate, smooth, and reflective. First, use a yellow marker pen to draw hatching to express the yellow plastic material. Strokes should be smooth, the gradations of light and shade should be general, and white space should be left appropriately within the highlight part, as shown in Fig.5.81.

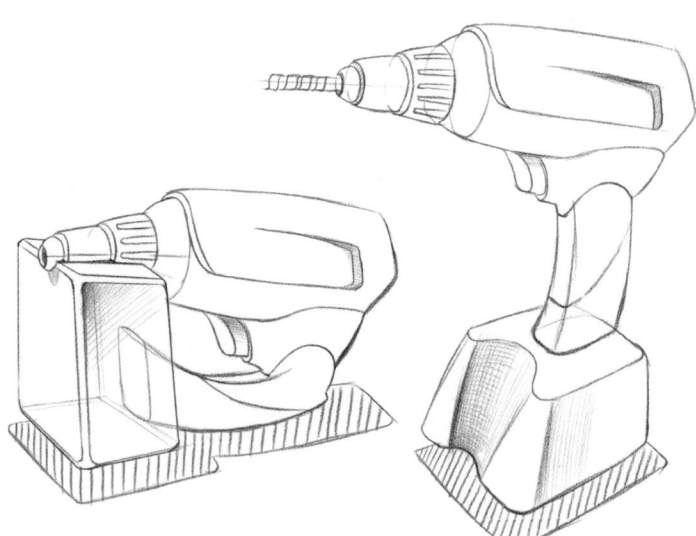

Fig.5.78 Outline sketch with detailing

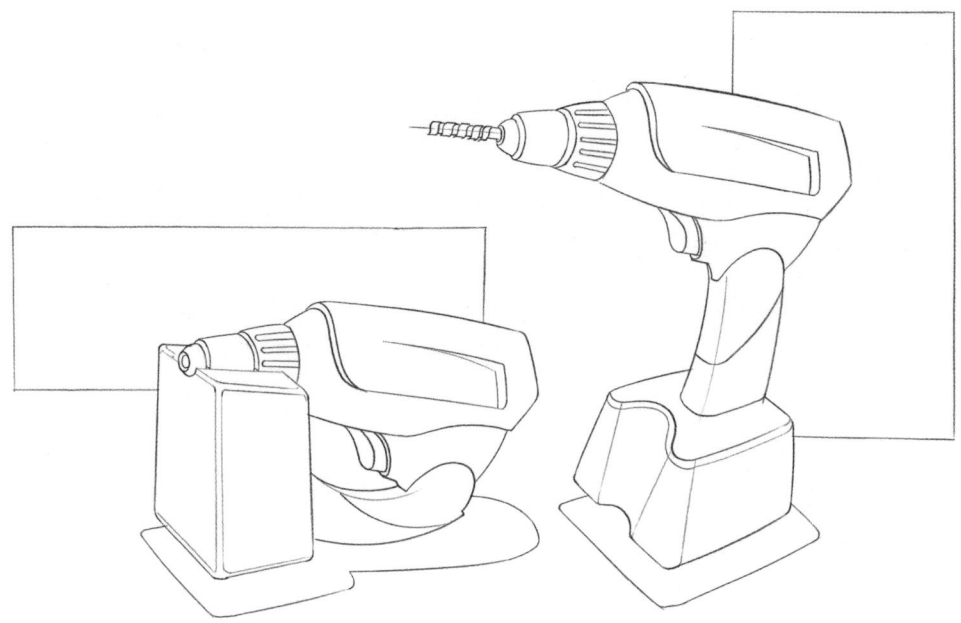

Fig.5.79 Outline sketch

Use gray and black marker pens to express black plastic. For the presentation of black plastic, it is not completely painted with a black marker pen, but a gray marker pen is used to present the light and shade changes of the black plastic. The light and shadow effects are expressed in a layered and organized manner. In addition, the overall tone of black plastic should be dark and close to black, as shown in Fig.5.82.

Step 4: Use marker pens to express the background and the cast shadow. The main product, background, and the cast shadow which complement each other and are mutually supportive to add to the integrity of the picture. A good background can make the picture more attractive. An appropriate cast shadow can make the main product more prominent. So, the choice of background color is particularly important. The background color should neither be too close to the main product color, nor too dark or too obtrusive. You can choose complementary colors, such as red, green, orange, blue, yellow, and purple for contrast. Finally, complete the rendering of the foldable and portable electric drill, as shown in Fig.5.83.

Instance Analysis of Product Modeling Design

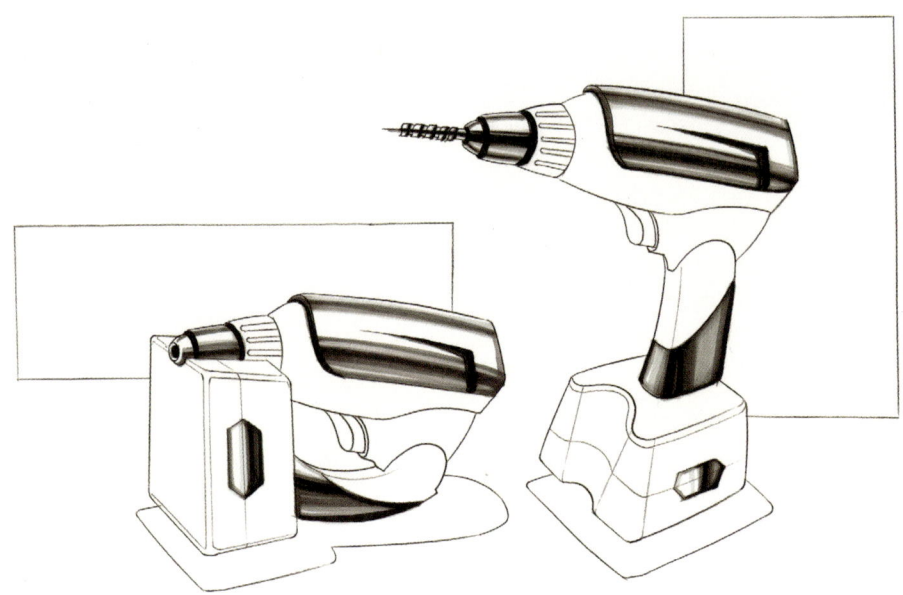

Fig.5.80 Detailing of metal surfaces with marker pens

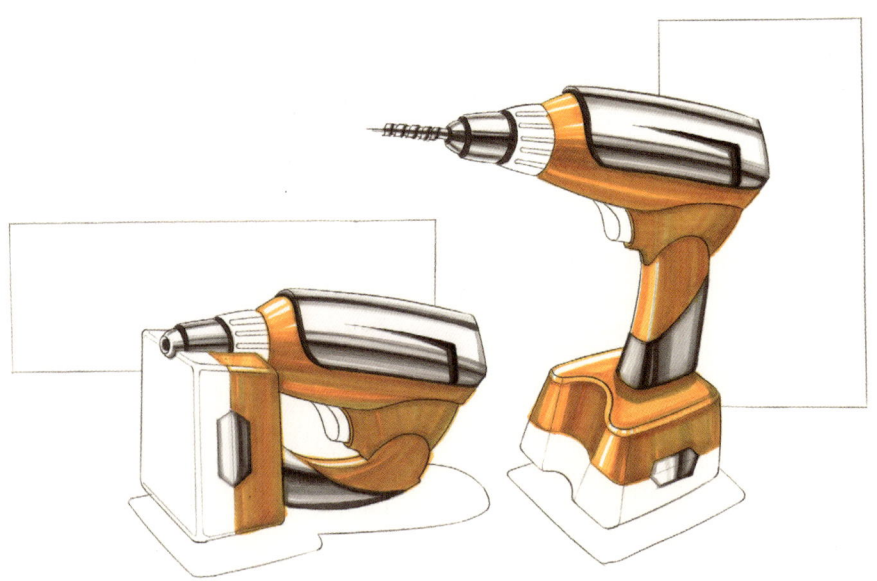

Fig.5.81 Detailing of yellow plastic surfaces with marker pens

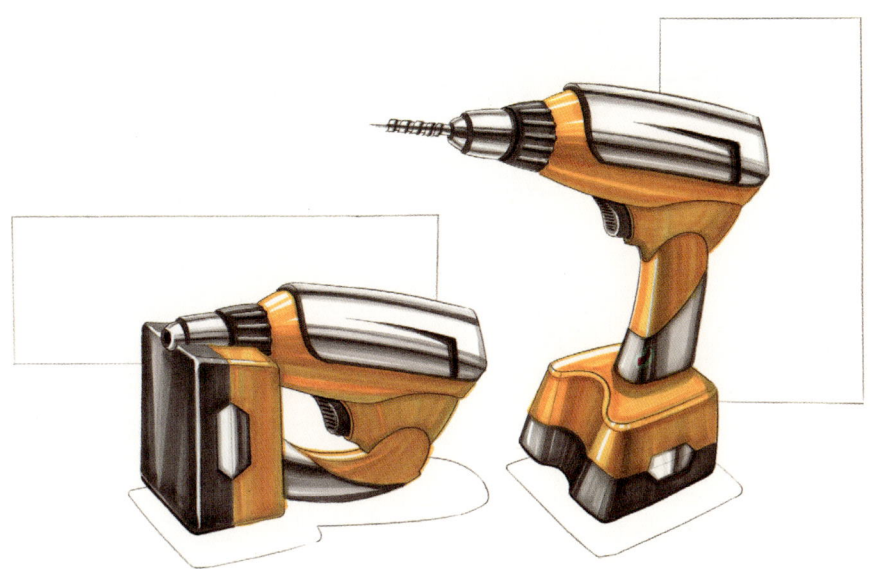

Fig.5.82　Detailing of black plastic surfaces with marker pens

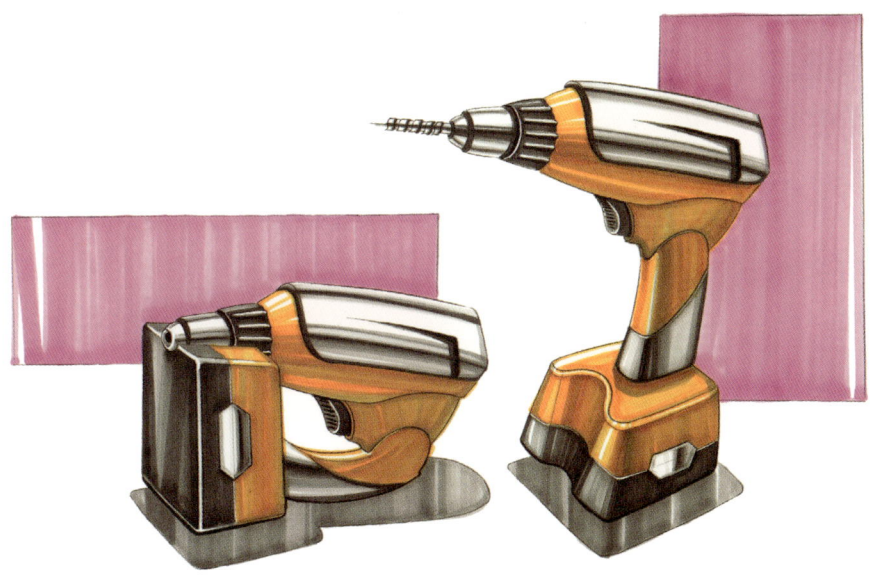

Fig.5.83　Detailing of background and shading effects with marker pens

Instance Analysis of Product Modeling Design

Instance Analysis of Product Design for medical and Rehabilitation Equipment

Medical and rehabilitation equipment products include medical instruments, medical staff office, laboratory equipment, basic activities of daily living (BADL) device, rehabilitation facilities, etc. These types of products are characterized by use for specific professional purposes and have high functional requirements, and specific structure and manufacturing methods.

Rehabilitation equipment design

Rehabilitation equipment refers to equipment used by patients for rehabilitation training.

Rehabilitation equipment mainly includes exercise rehabilitation equipment, occupational therapy equipment, BADL equipment, etc. The materials are mainly steel, wood, plastic, etc. They vary in structure, shape, size, weight, and usage. Some of them can be simple and some can be overly complex, as shown in Fig.5.84 to Fig.5.87.

The advancement of technology has pushed forward the rapid development of medical and rehabilitation equipment, and various forms of medical and rehabilitation robots have been gradually developed, including rehabilitation robots, robots for old people and disabled persons, surgical robots,

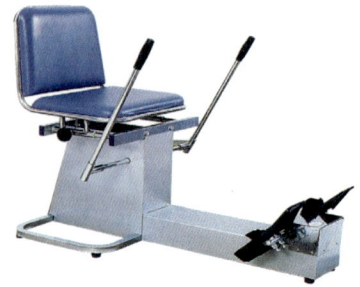

Fig.5.84   Rehabilitation exercise equipment

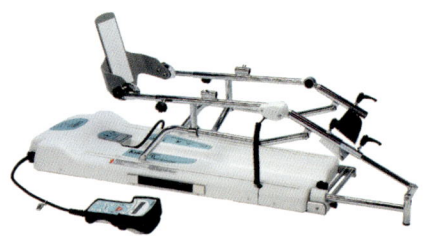

Fig.5.85   Physiotherapy equipment

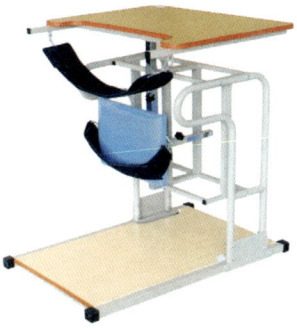

Fig.5.86 BADL rehabilitation equipment

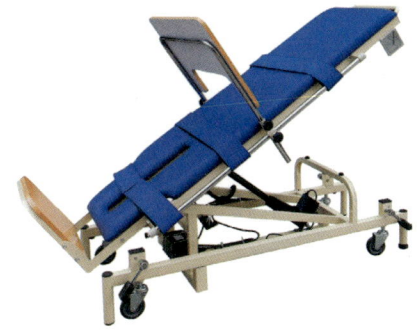

Fig.5.87 Auxiliary physiotherapy rehabilitation equipment

patient-care robots, chaperone robots, smart wheelchairs, etc. Among them, rehabilitation robots include upper limb rehabilitation robots, lower limb rehabilitation robots, intelligent rehabilitation robots, etc., as shown in Fig.5.88 to Fig.5.93.

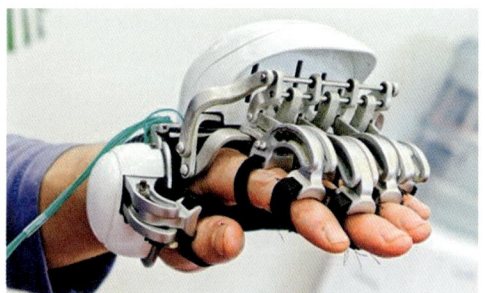

Fig.5.89 Surgical robot

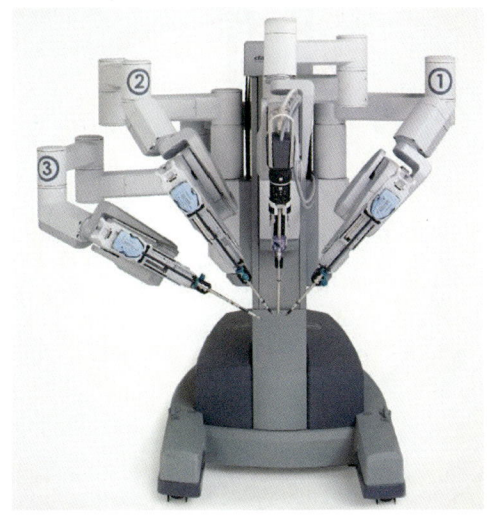

Fig.5.88 Nursing robot

Fig.5.90 Upper limb rehabilitation robot

Instance Analysis of Product Modeling Design 151

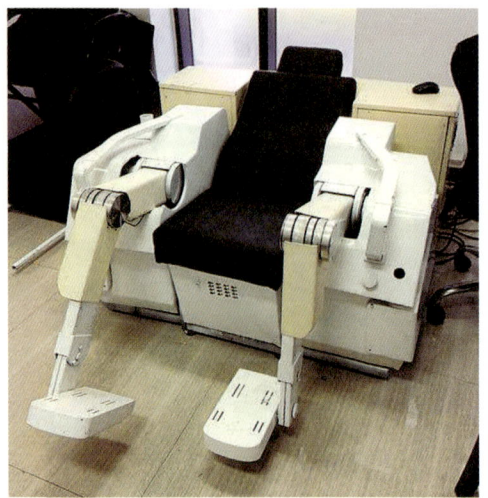

Fig.5.91 Lower limb rehabilitation robot

At present, the design of rehabilitation robots mainly focuses on fulfilling the function and not much attention is paid to its appearance design. In this regard, the modeling of the rehabilitation robot is not aesthetically pleasing and does not resonate with the brand image and corporate culture of the research and development company. On the other hand, the impersonal design of these rehabilitation robots always give people a mechanical, cold, and even frightening feeling. Therefore, patients may be reluctant to cooperate with doctors, causing great resistance to rehabilitation. Current rehabilitation products do not address the concern of users about the appearance of the product.

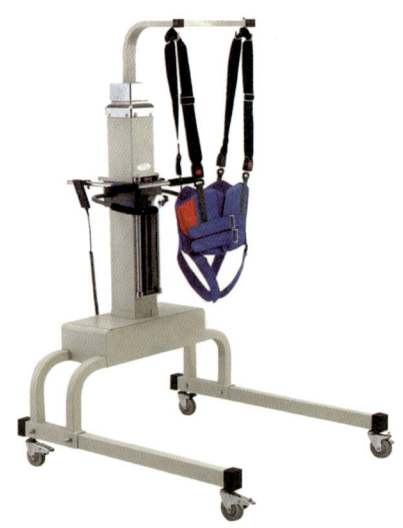

Fig.5.92 Intelligent rehabilitation robot (1)

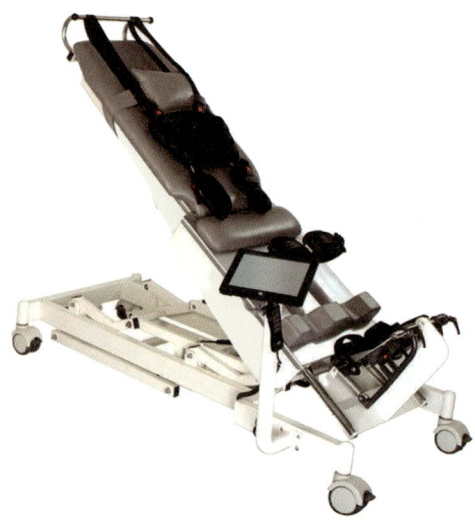

Fig.5.93 Intelligent rehabilitation Robot (2)

In response to this situation, in this section we take the appearance design of the rehabilitation robot as the theme, and design a series of themed intelligentre habilitation robots.

Through the image deduction of the letters "A" and "O", we get the corresponding bionic design and work out the design plan, as shown in Fig.5.94 to Fig,5.95.

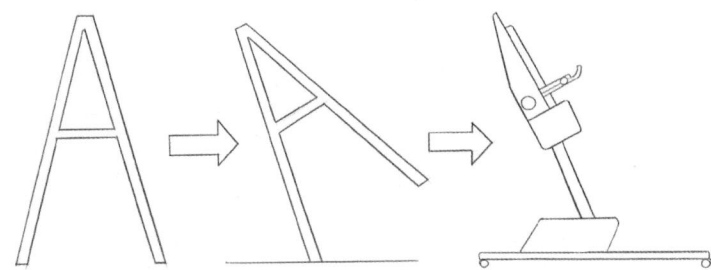

Fig.5.94 Bionic deduction with letter "A"

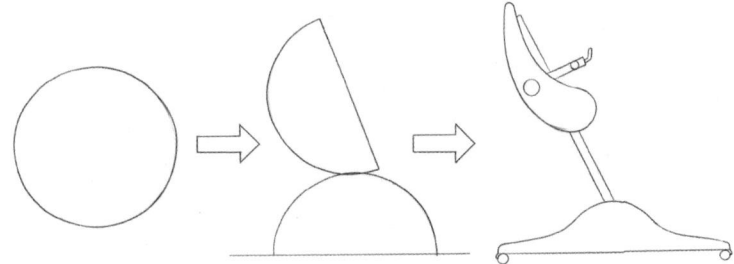

Fig.5.95 Bionic deduction with the letter "O"

Comparing them, the design plan of the rehabilitation robot obtained by the bionic deduction with the letter "A" as the prototype is analyzed. This rehabilitation robot has sharp edges and corners, which highlights the heaviness and segments of the rehabilitation equipment, giving the impression of being stable and reliable. Regarding the bionic deduction design based on the letter "O" as the prototype, the overall plan is sleek and concise, changing the cold, mechanized impression of medical equipment, and leaving a friendly, soft and attractive impression. The two rehabilitation robots are named after "Jiaoli" and "Yuanli", based on the design of these two different letters, as shown in Fig.5.96 and Fig.5.97.

Instance Analysis of Product Modeling Design 153

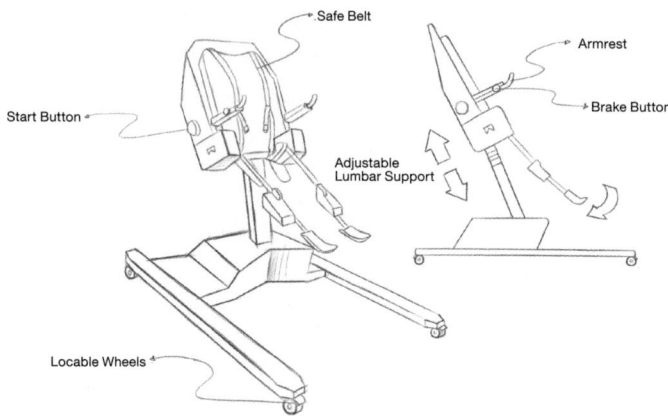

Fig.5.96 "Jiaoli" rehabilitation robot design sketch

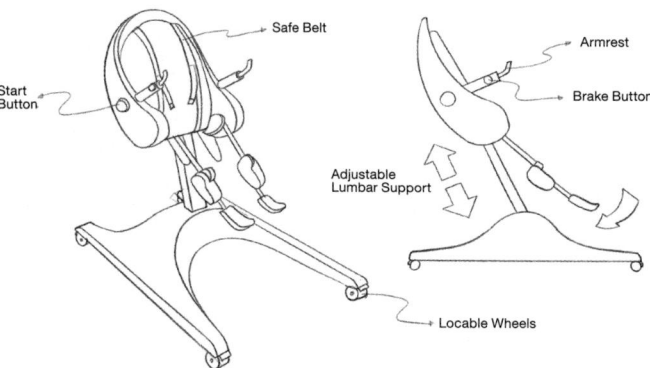

Fig.5.97 "Yuanli" rehabilitation robot design sketch

After completing the modeling design plan, the marker pen rendering can be drawn. The materials of these two rehabilitation robots are composed of metal and leather, including the painted part of the metal surface and the leather part of the back. To show the spray-paint effect on the metal surface, which is similar to the color effect of the plastic surface, you need to highlight the intrinsic color—the stroke should be neat and smooth, and appropriate white space can be left within the highlight part and reflected light part. To depict the leather effect of the back, it must fully reflect the smoothness, elasticity,

154 SKETCH LIKE A PRO

and set thread stitches of the leather. The specific steps are as follows.

Draw a modeling sketch. First, draw the final rendering based on the previous design sketch. You can highlight the theme by adding background text. Secondly, use simple and smooth lines to express the modeling outline sketch of the rehabilitation robot, as shown in Fig.5.98 and Fig.5.99.

Due to limited space, the specific drawing steps are not listed one by one. The final result is shown in Fig.5.100 and Fig.5.101.

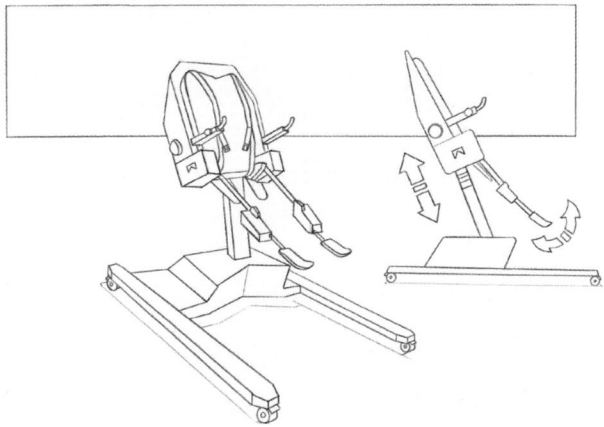

Fig.5.98 Modeling outline sketch "Jiaoli" rehabilitation robot

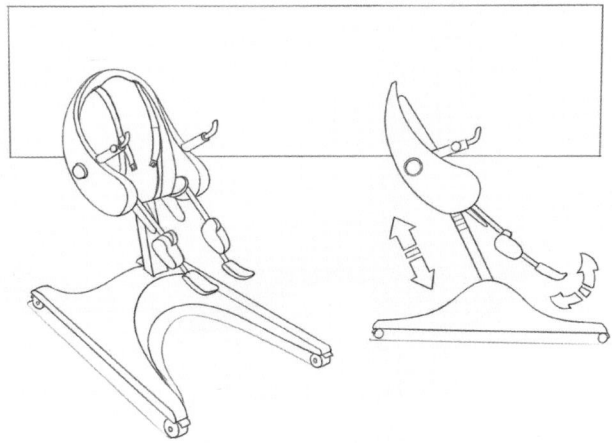

Fig.5.99 Modeling outline sketch "Yuanli" rehabilitation robot

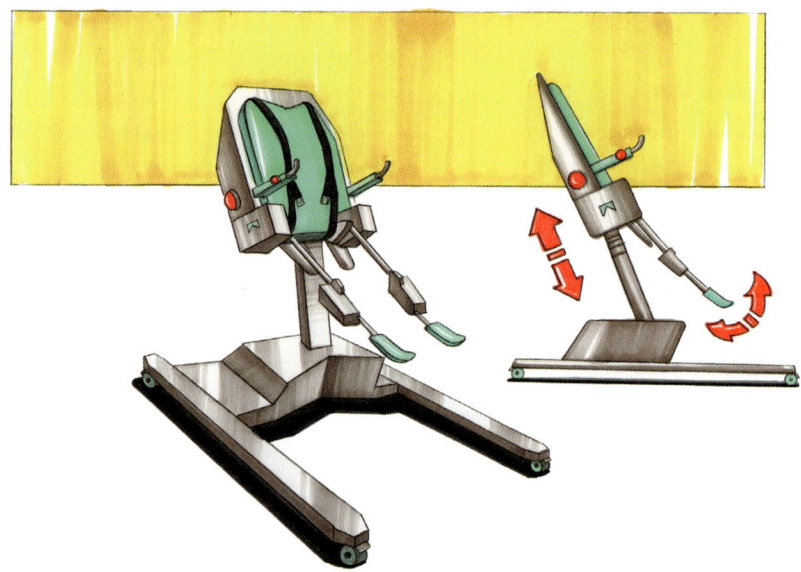

Fig.5.100 Final sketch of the "Jiaoli" rehabilitation robot design

Fig.5.101 Final sketch of the "Yuanli" rehabilitation robot design

Instance Analysis of Product Design for Public Facilities

Public facilities include restaurants, shops, lounges, libraries, museums, amusement facilities, display facilities, shopping facilities, outdoor billboards, and signage equipment, etc. Such products feature practicability, and have high functional requirements, and high frequency of use. In addition, they must be adaptable for indoor and outdoor environmental requirements.

Shopping cart design

Shopping cart refers to a kind of trolley that is convenient for customers to carry selected commodities in large self-assisted stores such as supermarkets and department stores. The shopping cart has a single-tray structure and a multi-tray structure, which can store different commodity categories. Sometimes, shopping carts are designed with children's seats and even with toy cars, as shown in Fig.5.102 to Fig.5.107.

Fig.5.102 Single-tray shopping cart (1)

Fig.5.103 Single-tray shopping cart (2)

Instance Analysis of Product Modeling Design

Fig.5.104　Multi-tray shopping cart (1)

Fig.5.105　Multi-tray shopping cart (2)

Fig.5.106　Shopping cart with plastic toy car (1)

Fig.5.107　Shopping cart with plastic toy car (2)

The shopping carts have not only made the purchasing activity more efficient for the consumer, but also increased the transaction volume of businesses.

With the advancement of technology and the advent of the internet age, people are paying more attention to online shopping, which has severely impacted the offline physical stores. The key concern of physical stores is to consider how to improve the shopping experience and let consumers feel relaxed, happy, and convenient when shopping in physical stores. Applying modularity and intelligence to the shopping cart has become a highlight. So, in this section we has design a modular smart shopping cart.

At present, the shopping carts in the market are mainly frame type, as the structure is simple, strong, easy to operate and easy to store, and the cost is relatively cheap. Therefore, this case uses the frame structure as an example and adopts a modular design concept to provide businesses with different forms of modular combinations. Single-tray structure, double-tray frame structures, and child seats can be added and combined according to different needs of different people. In this way, one shopping cart can be used for multiple purposes and save money for businesses, as shown in Fig.5.108.

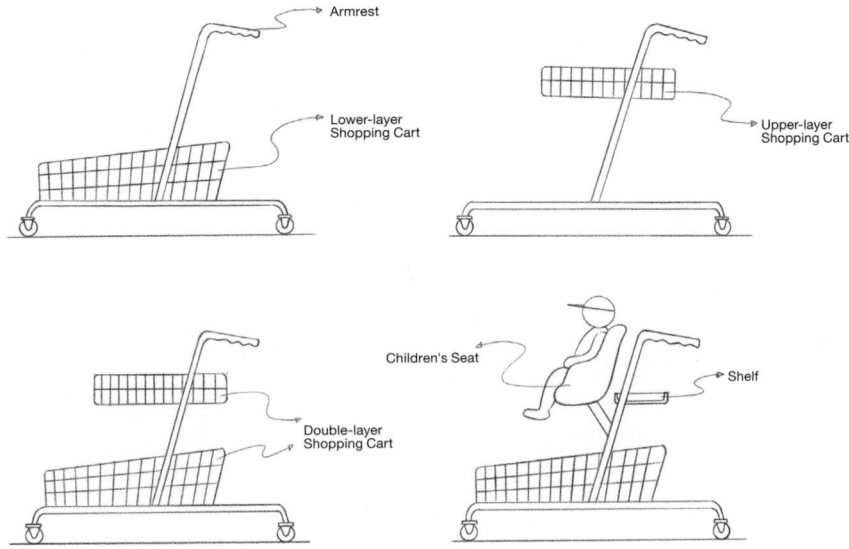

Fig.5.108 Modular shopping cart design

We can determine the basic modeling of the shopping cart by analyzing the modular construction. Then, complete the various components of the smart shopping cart, including intelligent e-shopping screen, product placement, frame structure, child seat position, etc. Finally, draw a sketch of the modular smart shopping cart design scheme, as shown in Fig.5.109.

The design sketch shows that the modular smart shopping cart is mainly composed of metal and plastic. We now draw the final renderings. The specific steps are as follows.

Instance Analysis of Product Modeling Design 159

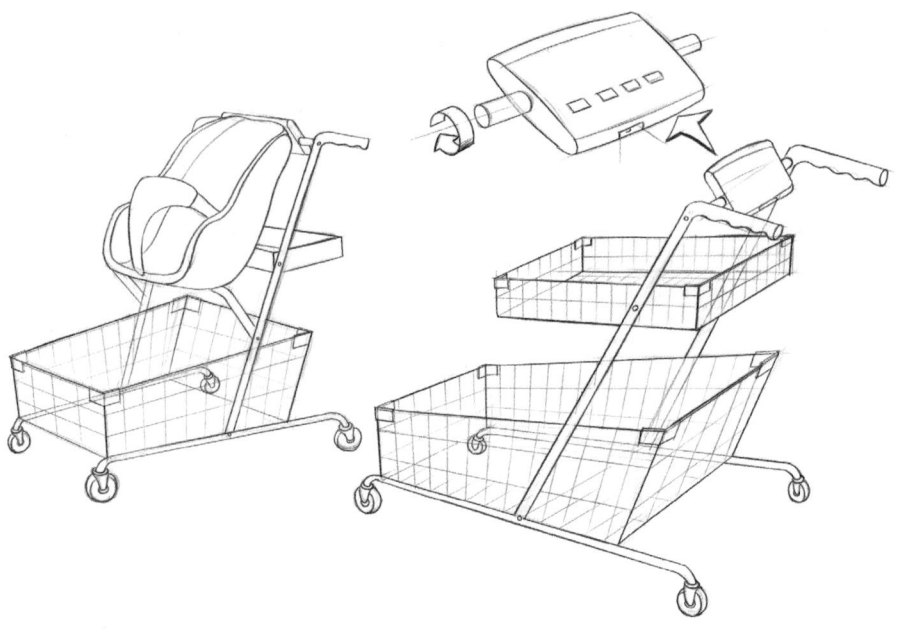

Fig.5.109 Schematic drawing of modular smart shopping cart design

Step 1: Draw the final outline rendering based on the existing draft. Firstly, grasp the composition and proportion of the picture. Secondly, highlight the theme by adding titles, backgrounds, and magnifying details. Draw the modeling sketch of the shopping cart with clear and smooth lines, as shown in Fig.5.110.

Step 2: Use gray marker pens to express the metal frame and wheels of the shopping cart. To make the overall contrast in the expression with marker pens, we need to make a number of thin lines for the metal frame of the shopping cart. This means that the color of the front and back should have different shades to reflect the sense of space. The overall tone of the wheel should be black and coordinated, as shown in Fig.5.111.

Step 3: Use red marker pens to show the plastic bumper and handle of the shopping cart. The marker pen emphasizes the intrinsic color of red plastic, and we should appropriately use chiaroscuro for expression, as shown in Fig.5.112.

Step 4: Use marker pens to depict the plastic child seat and shelf part of the shopping cart. The combination of yellow and blue is used here to make the shopping cart more colorful and more suitable for children. Highlight

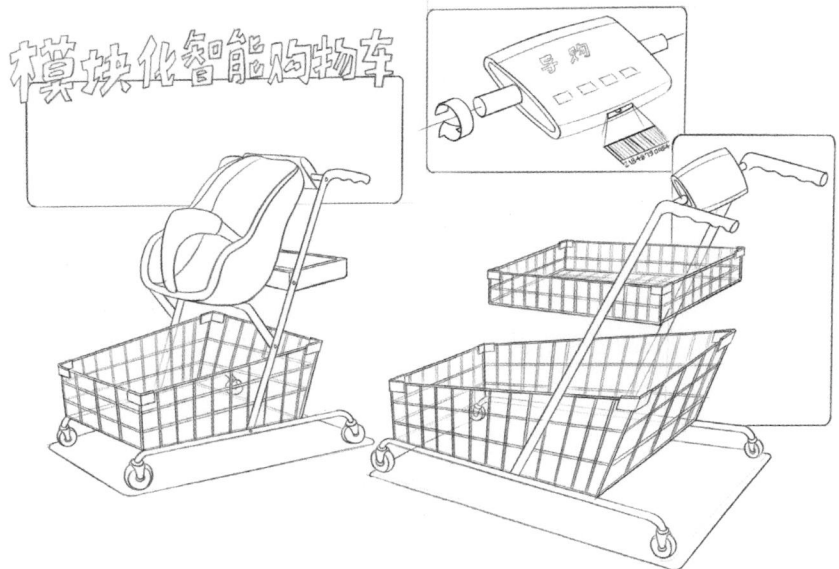

Fig.5.110　Outline sketch

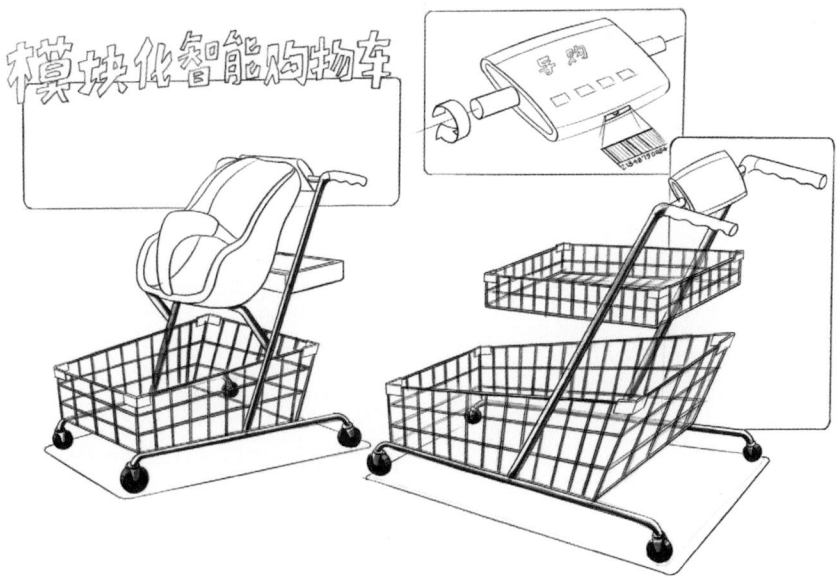

Fig.5.111　Detailing of metal frame and wheels with marker pens

Instance Analysis of Product Modeling Design

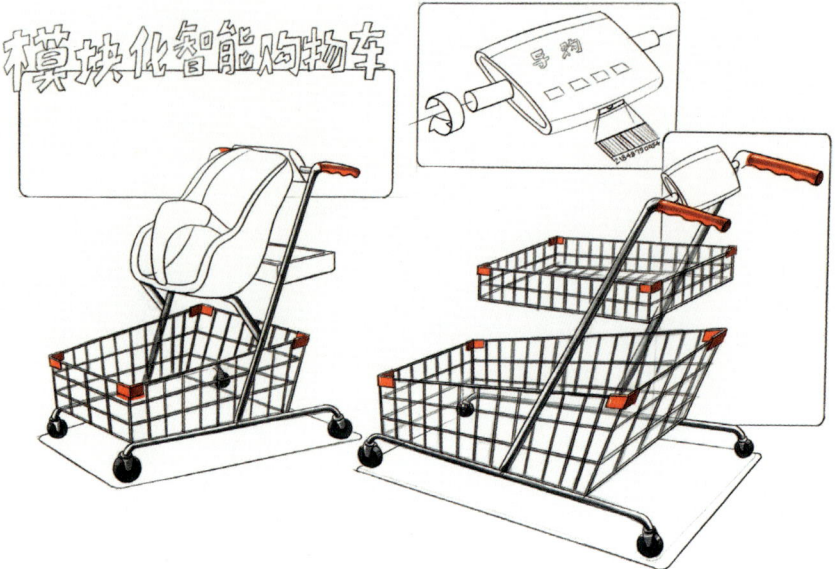

Fig.5.112 Detailing of plastic joint bumpers and handles with marker pens

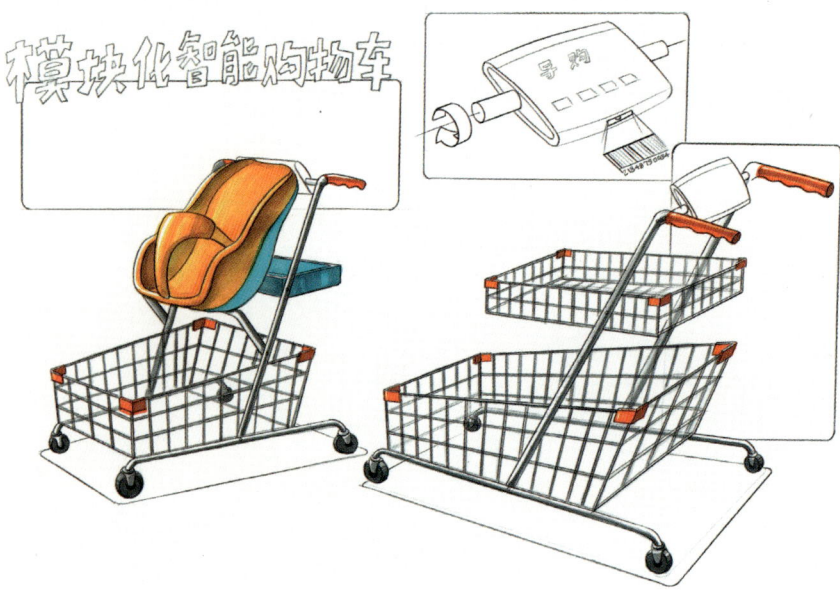

Fig.5.113 Detailing of plastic child seat and tray with marker pens

the intrinsic color of yellow and blue when expressed with marker pens, as shown in Fig.5.113.

Step 5: Use marker pens to express the material of the screen display. Blue marker pens can be used to draw hatchings to present the smooth and highly reflective surface, as shown in Fig.5.114.

Step 6: Use marker pens to express the title, the background and the cast shadow. The title, as an important part of the product rendering, can accurately describe the characteristics of the product and act as a reminder. It is coordinated and complementary to the main product, the background, and the cast shadow. In addition, the color and shape of the main product, the background, and the cast shadow should be coordinated with each other, as shown in Fig.5.115.

Fig.5.114 Detailing of glass surface of screen with marker pens

Instance Analysis of Product Modeling Design

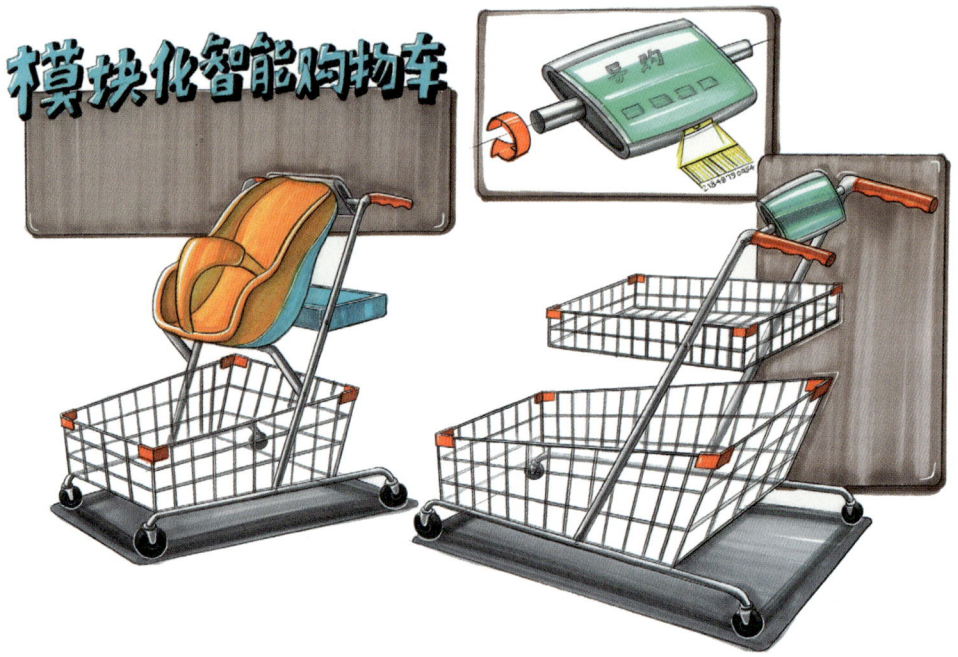

Fig.5.115 The completed final sketch

Instance Analysis of Product Design for Transport

Transport products include bicycles, electric bicycles, motorcycles, balance bikes, sedans, sports cars, SUVs, MPVs, buses, agricultural vehicles, construction vehicles, railway vehicles, aircraft, ships, etc. Such products feature a wide variety, have high functional requirements, are updated regularly, and have become an indispensable part of human life.

Electric bicycle design

Electric bicycles are personal vehicles that use batteries as auxiliary energy sources, and are equipped with motors, controllers, batteries, braking devices, display instruments and other systems based on a bicycle structure. At present, there are many electric bicycle brands in the market with various models, such as bicycle-like designs, motorcycle-like designs, scooter-like designs, folding designs, etc., as shown in Fig.5.116 to Fig.5.123.

Fig.5.116 Bicycle design (1)

Fig.5.117 Bicycle design (2)

Fig.5.118 Motorcycle design (1)

Fig.5.119 Motorcycle design (2)

Instance Analysis of Product Modeling Design 165

Fig.5.120 Scooter design (1)

Fig.5.121 Scooter design (2)

Fig.5.122 Foldable design (1)

Fig.5.123 Foldable design (2)

In this section we try to personalize the design of electric bicycles from the perspective of appearance to give the user a personalized, exclusive, and diversified experience. This design extracts elements from "Land Rover" cars and "Harley-Davidson" motorcycles, such as the tilt and dynamics of the "Land Rover" car body and the tough and stable structure of "Harley-Davidson" motorcycles to design the electric bicycle, as shown in Fig.5.124.

The basic modeling of the electric bicycle can be determined after extracting the modeling elements. It is assumed that electric bicycles are mainly composed of plastic shells, metal frames and wheels, rubber cushions and tires. Finally, we draw the renderings. The specific steps are as follows.

Step 1: Draw the final outline rendering based on the existing draft. Set the composition, proportion, background, and cast shadow. Then, use simple and smooth lines to show the modeling of the electric bicycle, as shown in Fig.5.125.

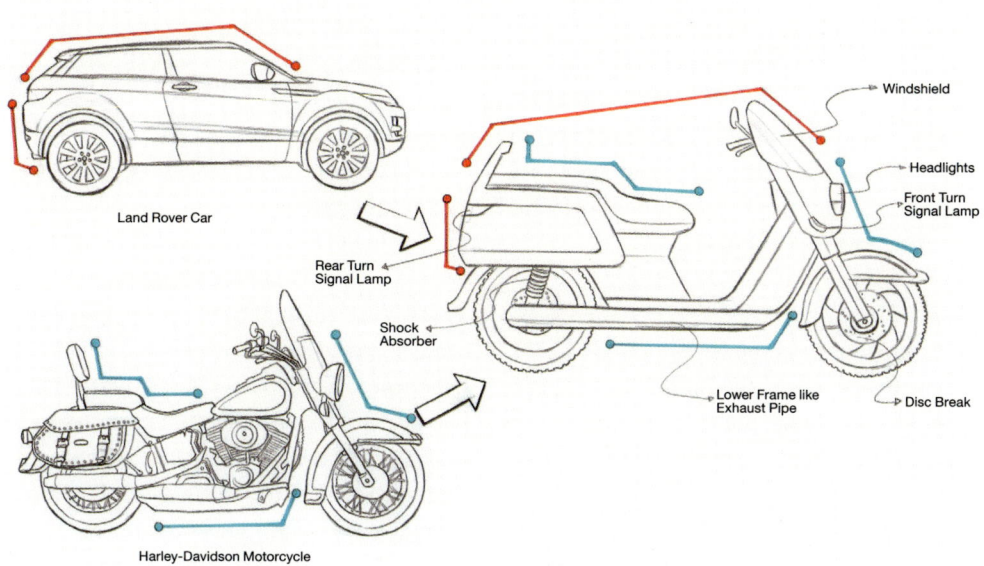

Fig.5.124　Design elements extracted for an electric bicycle model

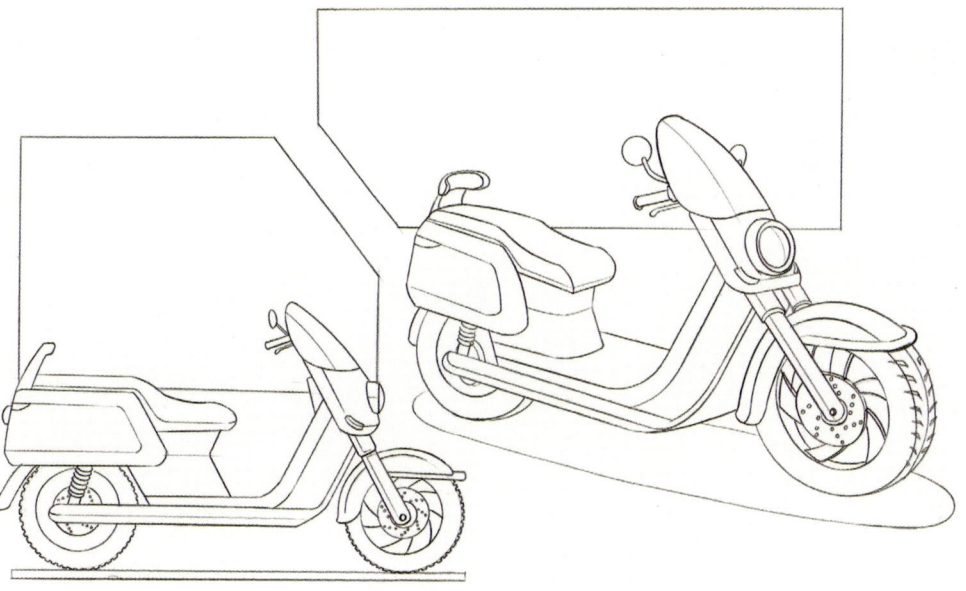

Fig.5.125　Outline sketch

Instance Analysis of Product Modeling Design

Step 2: Color the background with marker pens. First, analyze material features of each part of the electric bicycle, including light sources and the relations of light and shade, and then roughly distinguish the light side from the dark side with gray marker pens. Try to keep a good sense of the proportion in this step, as shown in Fig.5.126.

Step 3: Use marker pens to accentuate the chiaroscuro. As shown in Fig.5.127, overlay colors with marker pens of progressively darker colors to reflect the material characteristics of each part of the electric bicycle.

Step 4: Use marker pens to express the light fixture details. The highlight and reflected light parts are emphasized with marker pens to show the transparent surface of the glass in the headlight. Use white highlights for embellishment, as shown in Fig.5.128.

Step 5: Use marker pens to express the background and cast shadow. As the main body of the picture includes two views of the electric bicycle, the background part adopts the form of divided segments. Divide a square at 45°. Give the background more space to avoid the sketch appearing overcrowded or too rigid. Additionally, if the two sketches are separated, coordination and integration of features can be achieved more realistically. Light yellow markers are used to present the cast shadow, the color of which is close to the natural ground. Finally, complete the rendering of the electric bicycle, as shown in Fig.5.129.

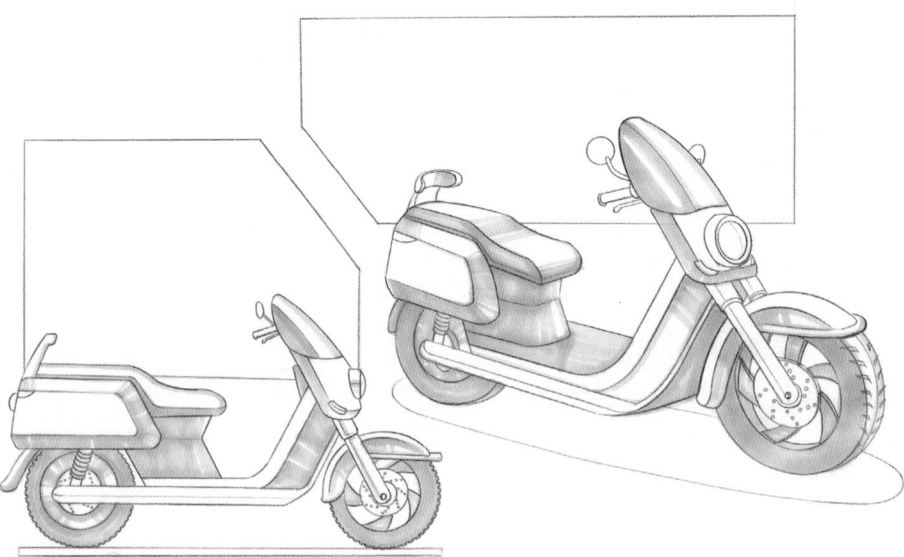

Fig.5.126 Background detailing done with marker pens

Fig.5.127 Background shading details done with marker pens

Fig.5.128 Headlight fixture details done with marker pens

Instance Analysis of Product Modeling Design

Fig.5.129 Background and shadow detailing done with marker pens

Instance analysis of hand drawn design of cars

Through the design of electric bicycles in the previous section, we have a preliminary understanding of the specific hand-drawing methods of transport products. Due to limited space, we are not listing out the steps of hand drawn designs of cars, one by one. The marker pen hand-drawn final renderings of three vehicles, cars, sports cars, and SUVs are shown in Fig.5.130 to Fig.5.132.

Fig.5.130 Car sketch done with marker pens

Fig.5.131 Sports car sketch done with marker pens

Fig.5.132 SUV sketch done with marker pens

Instance Analysis of Product Modeling Design **171**

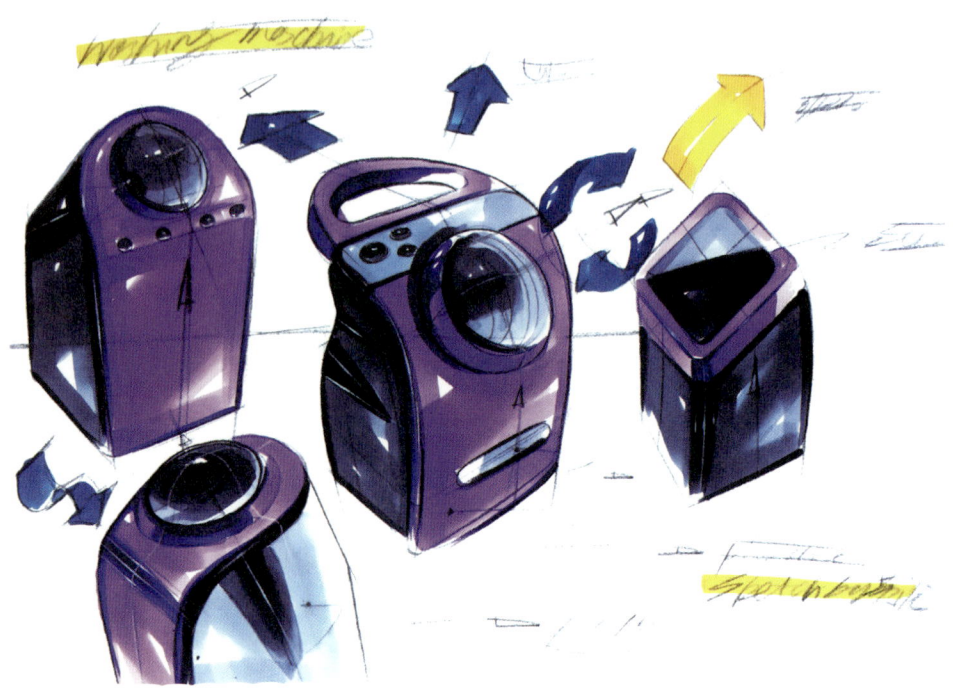
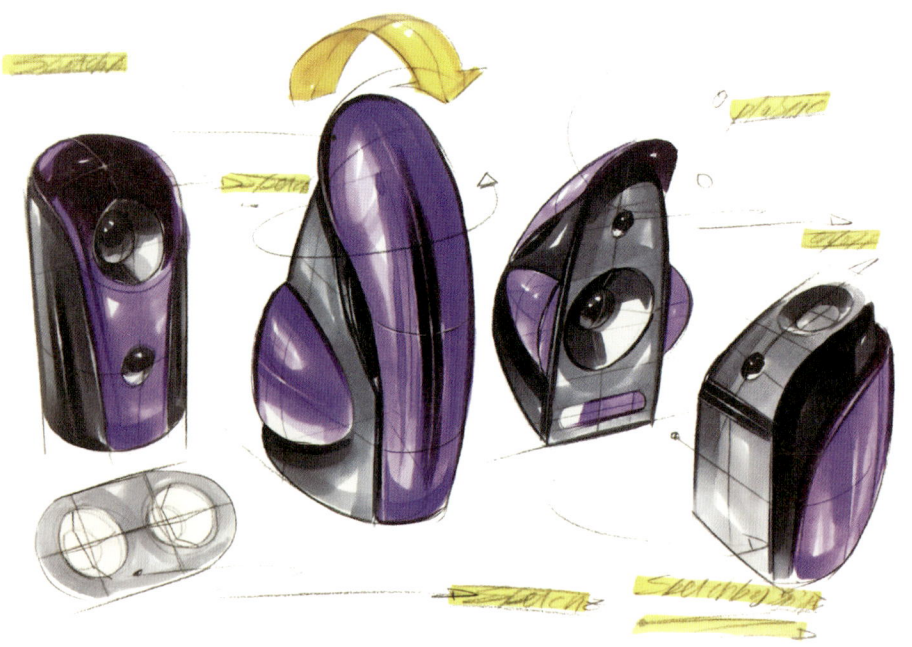

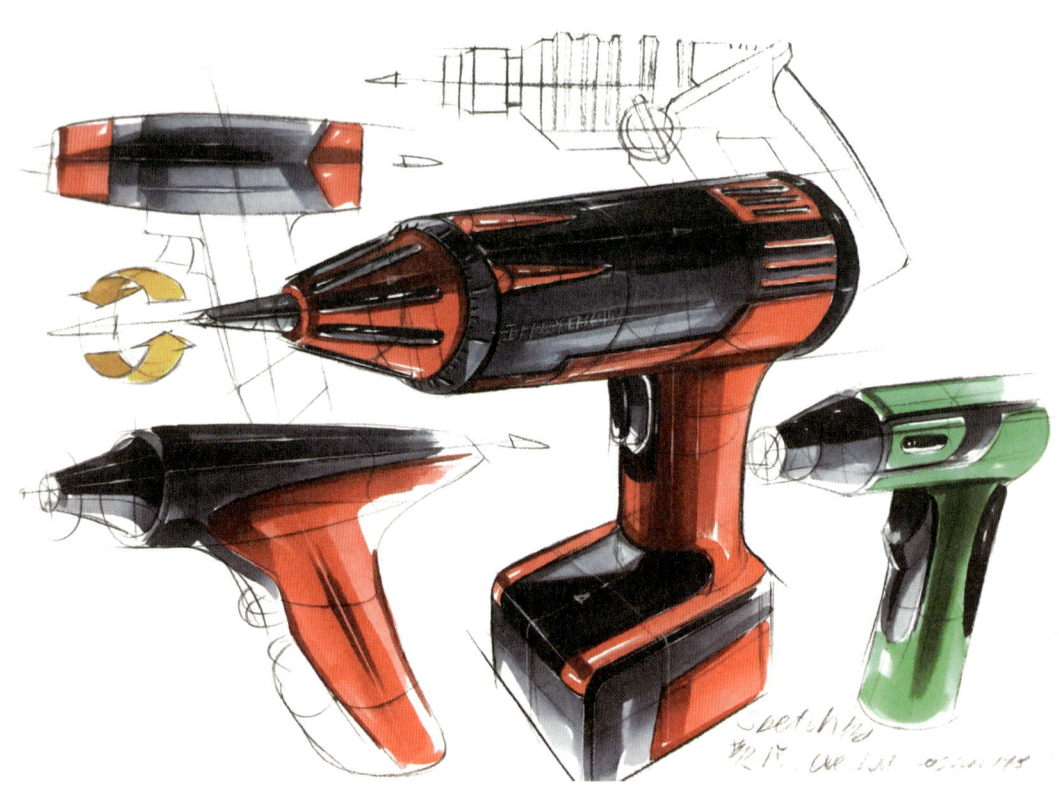

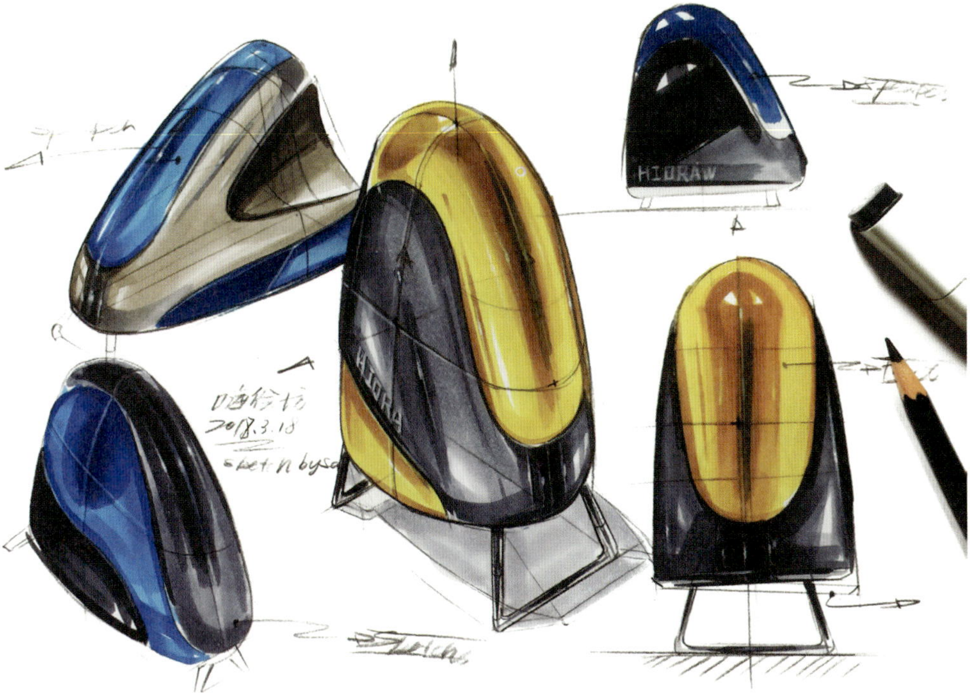

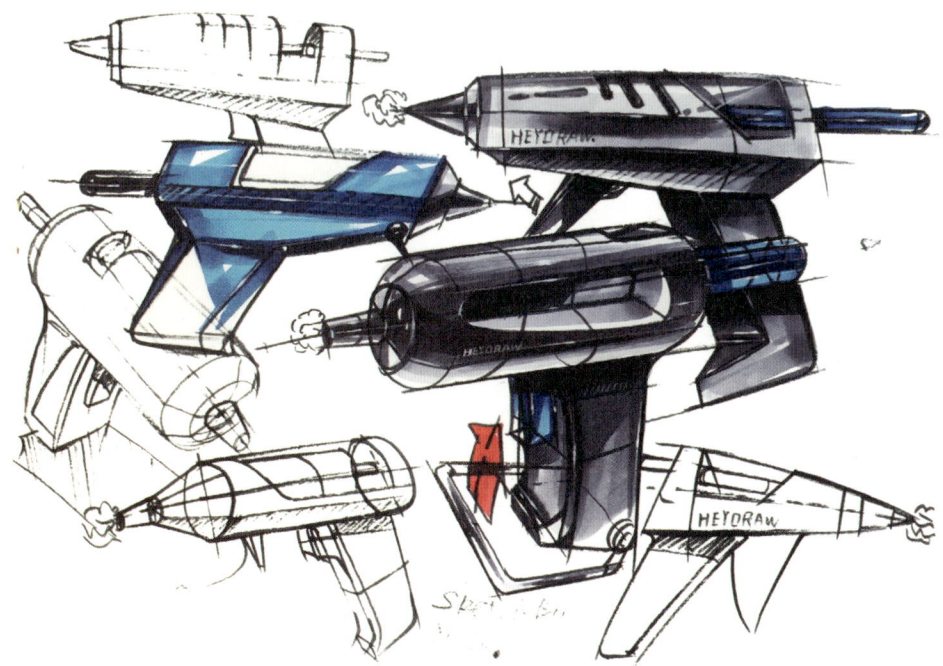

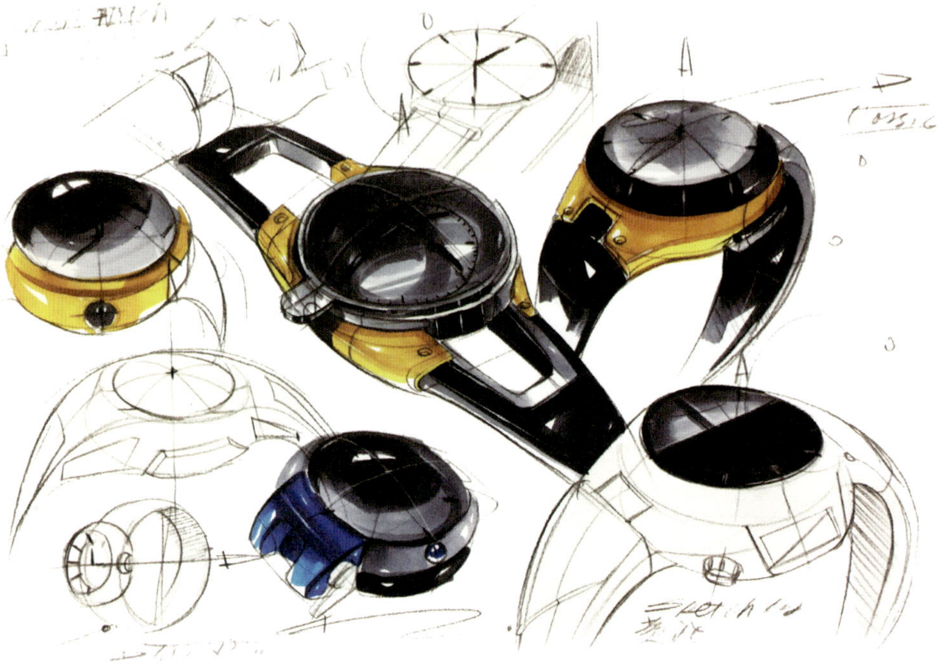

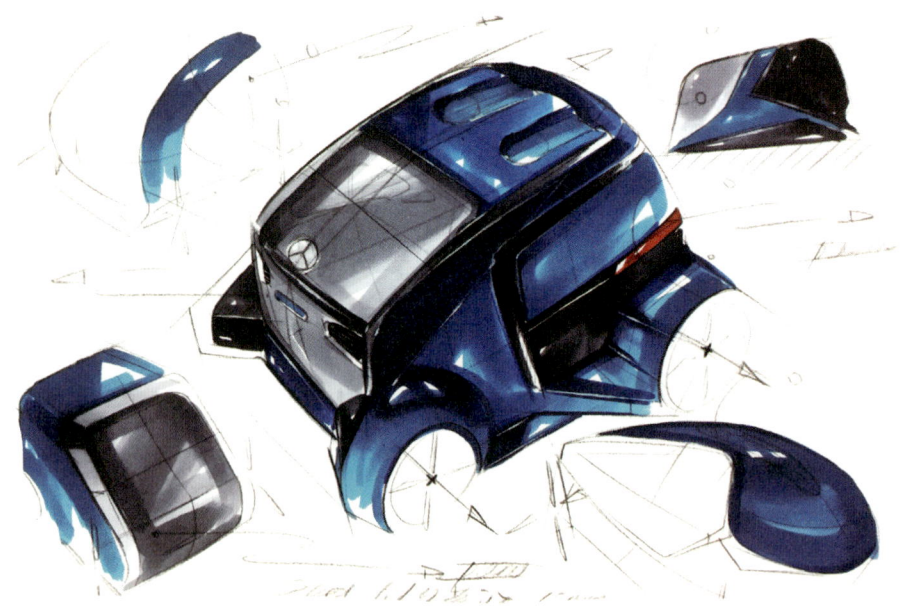

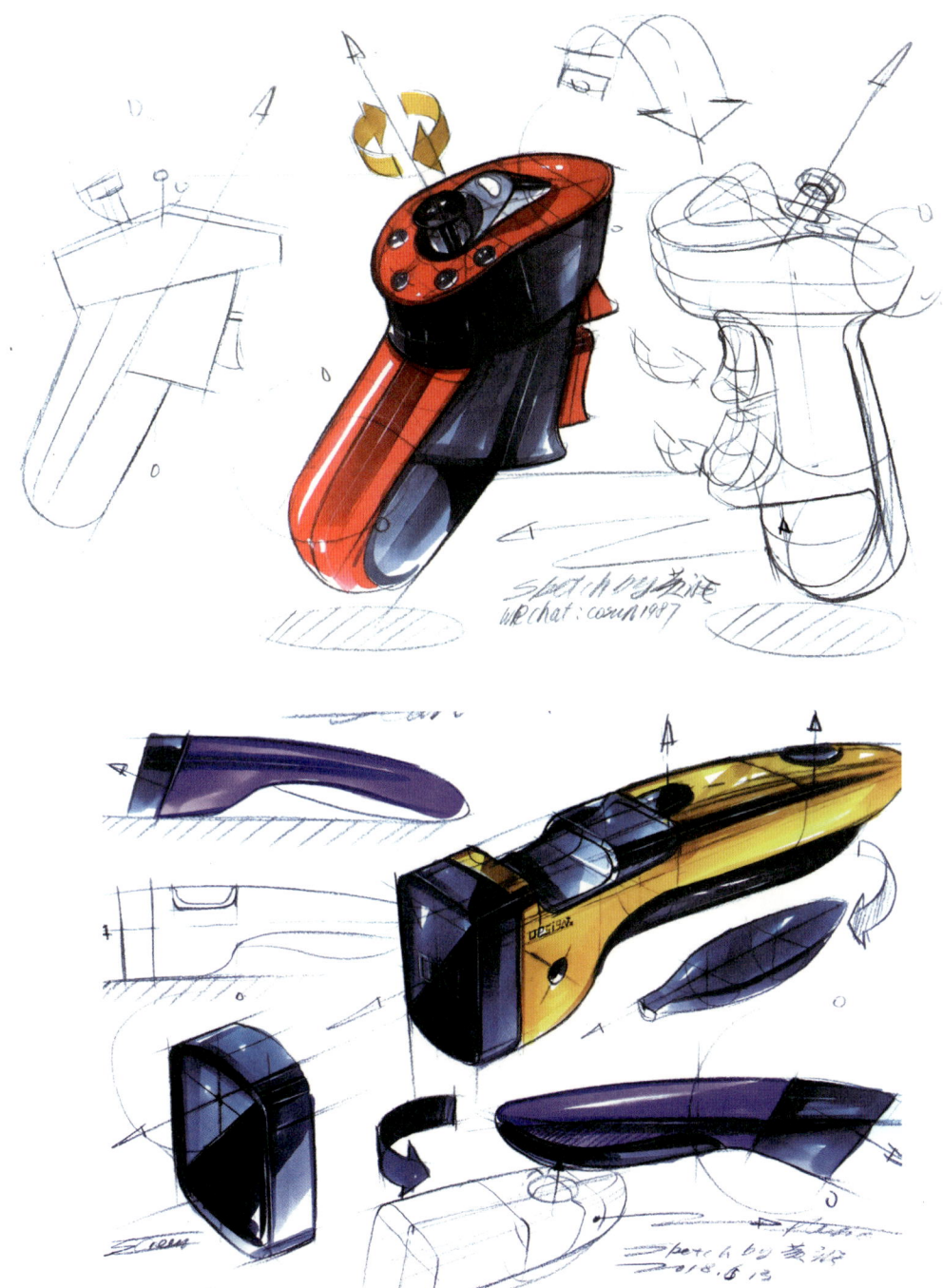

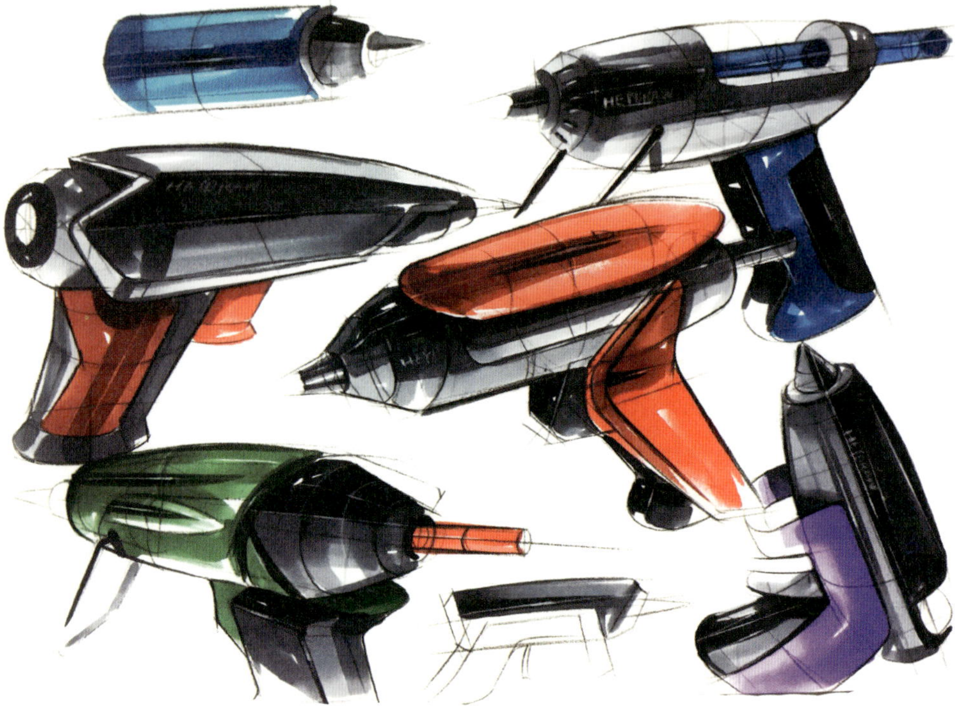

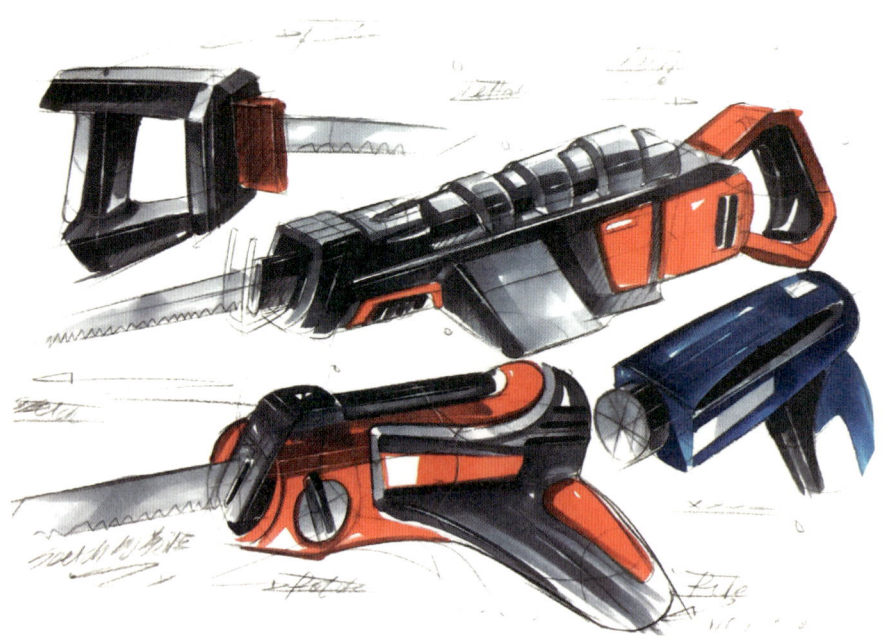